MOMENTS IN TIME

A BROKEN FIELD RUN THROUGH A LIFETIME OF BALTIMORE BASED SPORTS STORIES

By Paul M. Baker
with Foreword by Bill Tanton & Perspective by Vince Bagli

Printed and manufactured in
the United States of America

Cover Design, Story Editing & Book Composition by
Gary Adornato
Adeas Communications, Inc.
Baltimore, Maryland

Illustrations by
Michael Ricigliano

Memorial Stadium Cover Photograph by
Mike Smith
Aerial Views
Lisbon, Maryland

Library of Congress Catalog Card Number: 97-94565

ISBN: 0-9661217-0-8

10 9 8 7 6 5 4 3 2 1

To Connie,
Always there for me!

ACKNOWLEDGEMENTS

During this process I called on individuals and institutions who offered insights and remembrances that tilted my windmill and stirred me on. To Allen "Mack" Barrett, Stan Charles, Bill Gaertner, and Jim "Snuffy" Smith who read selections and gave encouragement, I thank you. To Joseph "Otts" Cascino, George Henderson, Harvey Kasoff, Coach Bob Lumsden, Marge (Wojcihovski) Woods, and Virginia Fowble for their thoughts and photos. To Richard Kucner for pointing a direction. And to all the people I interacted with in the book, mentioned or implied, thanks for the memories. I owe the most thanks to my editor Gary Adornato of Adeas Communications, Inc. who stated so convincingly, "Let's do it." My recollections were aided by the following entities:
- News Post Archives at UMBC
- McKeldin Library/Special Collections
  at the University of Maryland, College Park
- Special Collections/University of Baltimore Library
- Sunsource/The Sunpapers
- Enoch Pratt Free Library
- Mt. St. Joseph's High School Yearbooks
- Wheeling Jesuit University Public Relations Dept.
- Paul Baker/Photo Collection
- Pittsburgh Post Gazette Archives

ABOUT THE AUTHOR

Paul Baker was a successful, winning basketball coach at Towson Catholic, Baltimore University and Wheeling College in the 60's and 70's. His teams were noted for their defense and aggressive style.

Growing up in Baltimore he played in the City sandlots, lettering in football and baseball at Mt. St. Joseph High School and playing basketball, baseball, and golf at Baltimore Junior College and Washington College. He graduated from Washington College with degrees in Sociology and History.

Currently he edits the "Insights" basketball newsletter, appears on local radio talk shows, and hosts annual basketball dinners and bus trips. He is the Director of the Baltimore area Five Star Basketball Camp.

In addition, Baker begins his 17th year with the Atlantic Coast Conference as an Observer of Basketball Officials. He also worked as an NBA scout for six years.

The author lives in Cockeysville, Maryland with his wife of 33 years, Connie Peddicord Baker. They have three grown sons, Stephen, Gregory, and Nicholas, plus a new grandson, Jacob.

This is his first published book.

FOREWORD
By Bill Tanton

Paul Baker has written a remarkable book that will arouse a lot of nostalgic stirrings, particularly within the hearts of sports-minded people of my generation – the ones that grew up in Baltimore in the 40's and 50's.

That's when Baker was coming of age in the West Baltimore neighborhood of Irvington, home of Mt. St. Joseph's College High School, which the author attended. Baker not only recalls his earliest exposure to sports events there; he goes further back, to trips with his father to Memorial Stadium to see baseball and football games in the early 40's.

The most amazing thing about the book may be Baker's total recall of things that happened a half century ago. He seems to have remembered the uniform colors of every team he ever saw or played for. He recalls the football attire of the typical Irvington sandlot kid like himself, right down to the blue Cub Scout belt and its gold buckle.

He revived in my mind the long ago abandoned sports page practice of using dotted lines in photos to show the arc of a long pass, or the route a ball carrier had traveled on a long run. He writes about an overage bully – a ringer, as Baker puts it – who delights in beating up the younger players on Paul's team, only to get his comeuppance in the end. How many of us can remember a similar experience of our own, when the bully won and walked away unscathed?

It shouldn't surprise anyone who knows Paul Baker that he has such an amazing memory. He has been telling stories for all these years, and telling them with the same sort of detail.

It adds immeasurably to the book that Paul was no passive youth, simply sitting in the stands, taking it all in. As we might have guessed, Baker was what is now described as proactive. He plunged in full speed ahead when big league teams paid occasional visits to Baltimore. He sat on the bench of the Philadelphia A's with their legendary owner, Connie Mack. He shagged flies in the outfield when Hall of Famer Bill Dickey and the Yankees came to town. There he was in the dugout again when Ralph Branca and the Dodgers played in Baltimore. The sort of chutzpa that later helped Baker to become a college basketball coach was in place early on.

But the book is at its best when Baker is telling us about the people he actually played with and for, and about players he coached. And the images - my, oh my, how did he ever dig up some of those priceless old black and white photos? The picture of the late Mt. St. Joe coach, Vic Wojcihovski, is a dead ringer, with all its masculine appeal, for today's Sean Connery. The picture of the late basketball ref, Charley Eckman, whistle in his twisted mouth, is a classic. And how about that young, lean basketball hero of the old Baltimore Bullets, player-coach Buddy Jeannette? That one really transported me in time, since Jeannette is now 80 years old and a member of the Basketball Hall of Fame in Springfield, Massachusetts.

Baker writes personal reminiscences of Nick Schloeder, recently retired after a long and distinguished career as a teacher and coach at Gilman School, and of Ray Mullis, the late Cardinal Gibbons basketball coach. There is a long chapter on the former world champion boxer from Baltimore, Vince Dundee, and his friend, Paulie Mugavero – who happens to be Paul Baker's father.

Baker shows the reader his on-paper, on-the-record predictions that Muggsy Bogues and Grant Hill, as high schoolers, would blossom into top college and NBA stars. Before Hill graduated from high school in Northern Virginia, Baker wrote that this son of former football star Calvin Hill would become the greatest player ever to play for Duke, which he is. There is an illuminating chapter on Dunbar High product Dicky Kelly, who, in his late twenties, played for Baker at Wheeling College, and who, Baker says, would have been as good as any of the Dunbar stars who went on to star in the NBA, if only Kelly had come along ten years later.

My favorite chapter is about Howie Pyle, the late, colorful trainer at the University of Baltimore, where Baker also coached. The author, once again calling on his talent for detail, describes Pyle perfectly, down to "the dab of orange peroxide in the front of his hair" and two tape cans he always carried, filled with National Premium beer. I knew Howie well and I liked him, but I have often wondered how a writer could describe him without embarrassing his survivors or diminishing the man's contributions as a trainer dedicated to his athletes. Baker figured that out. He concludes that Pyle "gave more than he took" at B.U. The chapter, as the author says, provides "a vivid memory of days gone by."

This highly personal book will unearth hundreds of memories long thought forgotten. It did for me.

PERSPECTIVE
By Vince Bagli

No doubt, the biographies of MacArthur and Truman and Colin Powell have earned higher literary status – but I've never been more entertained than during the two hours I spent reading the anecdotal account of the adventures of Paul Baker.

There have to be legions of people from thirty-five to ninety, and youngsters too, who'll wonder how one guy could have woven so many ambitions, experiences, and accomplishments throughout one lifetime.

The kid from Irvington was born a dreamer! He wanted to play ball – to coach – to teach – to write – to be published, and, as much as anything, to be recognized for his entrepreneurial skills.

It's hard to say what he's done best.

He showed up, 145-pounds, but brash and determined to play two years on Mt. St. Joe's football team.

He taught history and coached basketball during the best stretch ever enjoyed at Towson Catholic. Then for four years at Baltimore University and nine years at Wheeling College, whose moribund sports program he elevated in that school's best years.

"The Bake" has always been a good story teller and

though you miss the passion in his voice and wild gesturing with his arms, he's even more entertaining when you read his written word.

If you've played golf at Clifton Park – you'll love Paul's impressions of Baltimore's oldest public course and the characters who show up there almost every day. The atmosphere is different than at most courses, but it's a beautifully maintained layout which guarantees a good score if you can handle the traffic connecting Harford and Belair Roads and some tough par threes.

The stories about boxing champion Vince Dundee, 1940's basketball leader and later Hall of Famer Buddy Jeannette, of football's Vic Woods, Paul's high school football coach, and Calvin Hill, the NFL star, as well as scouting reports on Grant Hill, Calvin's son, and the most unlikely of NBA leaders, 5'-3" Muggsy Bogues – all of these accounts have personal touches never before revealed.

Paul reached most of the standards he set for himself but admits that the opportunity to motivate and instruct during his Saturday morning practices gave him almost as much satisfaction as many of his basketball and baseball memories.

Besides his real job of selling insurance and helping with estate planning – the rest of us stay involved in his world, playing golf with him many times a year and by participating in his variety of seasonal entrepreneurial extravaganzas.

Paul doesn't just load up the van with four to six friends for a basketball game at Towson, Morgan or Loyola. He rents a bus, piles forty guys on-board, gives 'em a boxed lunch and drinks, and heads for the Palestra in Philly for Temple against Princeton or the U.S. Air Arena for Georgetown and Villanova. This costs each customer/fan about 40-bucks – but the bus, lunch, and game package is bookended by a Baker monologue, punctuated by questions on the state of the sport, going to and coming from the arena. Invariably, this feature is the highlight of the junket.

Then quarterly, the bus crowd and hundreds of other disciples he's attracted over the years, receive copies of his "*Basketball Insights*" publication – a kind of a one-man compiled and edited *Sporting News*.

Although opinionated on everything, Paul is not pedantic, and is, in fact, a good listener who might use one of your theories to put a different spin on one of his own.

The playing and coaching and teaching of American History have brought success and good memories but Paul Baker's intensity drives him to publish more of his stories, and to fill the Little Italy banquet hall for his pre-NCAA basketball tournament prognostications dinner, and to dip into the high 70's at Clifton and Longview.

If there's anybody, anywhere with more determination than this dynamo – he hasn't come my way!

Table of Contents

Section I

Experiences of My Youth

BALTIMORE'S MEMORIAL STADIUM
The Love Child Lives

"For over 50 years we have been magnetically drawn to her. . . from hero worship to near religious experiences, the stadium became the axis of the days of our lives."

It's Saturday, August 3, 1996 AD and once again I am going to a football game at Memorial Stadium. My first appearance on these grounds was 52 years ago, when at the age of nine, my father took me to the Army-Navy game. It was December 2, 1944. From then til now, many things in my life can be defined by the Stadium and its events. Thousands of Baltimoreans and their families have had similar experiences, but I never expected it to continue.

I was packed into a four-door Taurus with five young fanatics and by 4:00 p.m. we were locked, bumper to bumper, into the Eastern High School parking lot. Out come drinks, the food, the grills, the small talk and the nerf footballs and, all of a sudden, we have a giant love-in. After a cold beverage and a sandwich, I leave the gridlock to walk to the 33rd Street concourse.

Souvenir hawkers abound and the fans are beginning to congregate. The first Baltimore Ravens game is only a few hours away. Sitting on the steps of Eastern High School directly across from the stadium entrance, I observe the passing parade. The old Colt tradition will never be forgotten, but today these people are wearing purple. Ravens paraphernalia abounds everywhere. Is it wrong to switch one's love allegiance? It happens everyday in America, and today I was viewing the transformation. The sporting rabble – fathers and sons, husbands and wives, friends, lovers, and the tailgaters, all happy, spirited, and wearing purple – made my day.

Around 6:30 the humidity of a Baltimore August broke and a fresh breeze swept across the concourse. Boom box music from the parking lot wafted through the air. The word "love" kept popping into my brain and then it hit me, the stadium over the years is Baltimore's unabated and unrelenting "Love Child." We love her unconditionally. For over 50 years we have been magnetically drawn to her. We all have our own Colt and Oriole stories. From hero worship to near religious experiences, the stadium became the axis of the days of our lives. Sort of a Lourdes at 33rd Street.

Today the Love Child was clean and fresh again. Her adoring public poured in on cue and filled every seat. Sitting on the steps I began to reminisce:

December 2, 1944: Army-Navy. . . Wearing gabardine knickers on a freezing cold day. . . getting lots of splinters. . . hot chocolate and corned beef sandwiches from Nate's & Leon's on North Avenue. . . Cadets and Midshipmen marched into the stadium in an unending procession. . . You could see their freezing breath and feel their energy. . . They kept up a haunting, humming chant. . . Blanchard and Davis too much for the Middies. . . The bands and the bright uniforms were spellbinding.

July, 1945: Watching the International League Orioles play in the wooden stadium with no roof. . . Sitting in the bleachers with Joe Dembeck and his dad, hoping to catch a

4

Howie Moss home run. . . We always took our gloves. . . Admission was 50 cents.

Spring, 1947: Exhibition baseball, Yankees vs. Dodgers. . . 9:30 a.m. - I am on the field taking throw-ins from the outfield for Bill Dickey, the Yankee coach. I was wearing a black and orange tackle twill shirt with a homemade Oriole cap that I had produced at the Torsch and Franz Badge Shop on Park Avenue, the present site of the Omni Hotel (in those days there was no licensed apparel, so my cap was both rare and unique). During a pepper game Dickey hits one on the grain, a tiny crack appears and he gives me the bat. . . 10:30 a.m., I'm leaning on the cement retaining wall watching this tall, lean and mean looking Dodger fire pitch after pitch into

The Love Child in Full Bloom: On October 22, 1935 (the year I was born), 66,000 fans witnessed a Navy-Notre Dame matchup at Memorial Stadium. Vic Wojcihovski (my high school football coach) played for the Irish and among the spectators were Dr. Francis Bagli and his son Vince.
Photo: Courtesy of the Enoch Pratt Free Library, Baltimore, MD

this fat catcher's mitt. He is grim and sweating up a storm. We make eye contact a few times but say nothing. As he finishes this "simulated game," he looks right at me and flips me the ball. No smile, no talk, just the ball. It was Ralph Branca four years before Bobby Thompson. . . 11:00 a.m., ushers kick me off the field. . . Dickey and Branca were nowhere to be found.

One week later: It's high noon and I'm in my Oriole get-up, squeezing my claw mitt at the page fence in front of the Administration Building. The Philadelphia Athletics trot out wearing their blue jackets with white elephants on them. I try to squeeze through with them, to no avail, but as the last player passes through, a gentle hand touches my shoulder. I looked up to see a skinny giant with kind eyes. He was wearing a three piece suit with a celluloid collar and straw hat. He didn't say a word, he just nodded to the usher and in we went. He smiled as we made our way to the dugout where I stayed the whole game. I wore Russ Christopher's jacket. The tall guy still never said a word and he just smiled every now and then. I learned later his name was Connie Mack, who was 84 years old at the time. At the age of 12 these experiences gave me confidence and a feeling that anything was possible.

Fall, 1947: I worked all summer for Mrs. Ross, a neighborhood seamstress and saved up enough money to buy a season ticket to see a new football team called the Colts play at the Stadium. They wore drab green and silver uniforms and in the first game, we beat the Brooklyn Football Dodgers 16-7. It took two streetcars to get there from my house. I had permission and went to every game. I saw the Colts night game against the Otto Graham led Cleveland Browns where Billy Hillenbrand, the best broken field runner the Colts ever had, ran circles around the Browns.

1948-49: I watched City-Poly and Loyola-Calvert Hall on

Thanksgiving Day with neighborhood friends. Watching those teenagers play gave me the idea that maybe I could do it too. In 1949, as a high school freshman at Mt. St. Joe, I saw our team beat undefeated Patterson 24-0 in front of more than 20,000 fans. I was caught up in the frenzy and energy of this great game. It affected me more than any other event I ever experienced in this place. Coming into early manhood, I realized that I was going to one day play on that field. All my other experiences would be vicarious, but watching the St.Joe-Patterson game made me dream the dream.

1951-52: As a halfback for St. Joe, I played six times in the Stadium. I never scored a TD there, but I rushed for maybe 100-yards total. I dropped a 50-yard bomb vs. Loyola in one game, but I enjoyed every moment I spent on the field.

At this time, the Stadium was being rebuilt, right through the old foundation. The old Administration building went

The Changing Face: In the Spring of 1953, pillars were driven through the original stands, as the stadium's upper deck was added in anticipation of the big league Colts and Orioles. The Love Child never closed down during this construction, continuing to host area high school football games.
Photo: Courtesy of the Enoch Pratt Free Library, Baltimore, MD

7

down in favor of new seats and the upper deck enveloped the entire structure. The lights were brighter, the Orioles were getting ready for the American League, and the great moments kept on coming.

1954: The Orioles became a big league team. I went to Opening Day vs. the Chicago White Sox. The Love Child was clad in red, white and blue bunting.

1953-1956: Back came the Colts in blue and white with horse shoes on their helmets. The love flowed and the rabble was captivated with the team and the Stadium. It was easy to see that Baltimore was a football town as the Stadium became known as "the World's Largest Outdoor Insane Asylum." It was like a Woodstock love-in.

1958: My dad and I attended the Major League All Star Game. Seeing Willie Mays in person was very memorable. For the first time I realized that the black athlete was a phenomenon waiting to happen.

1960's: The Orioles came alive under Paul Richards and built the foundation for the 1966 World Champions. At this time, you could decide to go to any game, at the last minute, and still get a great seat. The franchise is blessed with some of the greatest players of modern time. . . immortals like Brooks and Frank Robinson, Jim Palmer, Cal Ripken, Jr., and Eddie Murray, just to name a few, and I saw them all in the Stadium. You can fill in your own blanks from your own Love Child file.

1970's: Living in West Virginia with all of our family still in Baltimore, we returned every Summer and I'd take my sons to see the Orioles. Also, we saw the spellbinding Colts-Raiders playoff game. My middle son Gregory was an especially avid fan, not to be deprived of his heritage. He loved Bert Jones and Eddie Murray.

1980's: We moved back to Baltimore and were neighbors of the Crowleys. My boys and the Crowley sons would go to the park early and Terry would let them roam the field, much like I did some 40 years ago with Dickey and Branca. The boys got to know Mark Belanger, Rick Dempsey and the Ripkens. We were at the Love Child the night Terry Crowley launched a Goose Gossage fast ball far into the night with the bases full, to beat the dreaded Yankees. We rushed home and the kids painted a quick sign and attached it to the Crowley garage door. It read, "Tonight the Crow Cooked The Goose!" I was so glad my sons got to experience the Baltimore feeling.

1980's: Larry Lucchino was a high school basketball player at Taylor Alderdice in Pittsburgh and he later played at Princeton. At Bob Cousy's Camp in New Hampshire I was his counselor and mentor. When he became an Oriole partner we were reunited and spent many hours reminiscing. I had carte blanche to Larry's box and we would go up in the middle innings and sit in those plush revolving seats. I called it the Imperial Box. I remember the Brady Anderson for Mike Boddicker deal and raising hell about losing Mickey Tettleton. I brought up friends and clients. It was a heady time at the Love Child and one of the crowning moments revolved around the visit of Queen Elizabeth and Prince Phillip. I saw them through the binoculars from deep in the right field bleachers. Two weeks later, Snuffy Smith and I visited Larry. It was a slow night against Seattle and we were talking hoops with Calvin Hill, father of Grant. He was one of Larry's lieutenants. When the waitress arrived we all ordered the #1 entre then sidled down to the front row of the Imperial Box. There we sat on a balmy Baltimore Fall night eating Filet Mignon, with baked potato and Caesar salad (What has baseball come to?). I swear I could still feel the warmth of the Queen's portly bottom through the crushed leather seats. Within two weeks in the Love Child, I had literally gone from the outhouse bleachers to the castle of the Imperial Box. It could only happen in Baltimore.

<u>1970's, 80's and 90's:</u>   Those Thanksgiving Day high school games have become a real "days of our lives" experience.   The press box has become a Who's Who of former players, coaches, writers, and long time fans – many who have come from out of town to be there. A few years ago, my friend Bill and I stayed in the press box after a Loyola-Calvert Hall game telling stories. We then climbed to the top of the Love Child which had now been vacated by both the Orioles and Colts. Taking a Swiss Army knife we cut the rope to the flagless flag poles in Sections 34 and 35, releasing the tarnished brass clips.   They went to a brass shop where they were cleaned up and inscribed, and later presented to two former Oriole and Colt executives – Mac Barrett and Ernie Accorsi. The Love Child Instinct came to the fore that morning.

My reverie is snapped by the clacking, quacking noises of the new era. Raven calls are resounding in the night air. The Stadium is filled to a frenzied capacity of 65,000 for an exhibition game in mid-Summer. The love affair is still alive. At halftime, the Baltimore Colt Marching Band gets its cue and a hush comes over the crowd as the band marches back onto the hallowed ground. It was a historic moment after a 12-year hiatus. Soon, the Colt Fight Song fills the air as old wounds bind and begin to heal. The fans erupt and goose bumps appear.

The past is alive, but it quickly gives way to the present as the chill of a Summer breeze carries a strange new noise – the Raven cackle – through the air from the far reaches of the Stadium. The new era has begun.

Being the oldest and only truly sober member of the tailgate crew, I become the wheelman and wonder out loud how these young men will share their own memories with their children.

In 1998, the Ravens will head to Camden Yards and their

much anticipated new stadium, leaving the Love Child tenantless once again. At that time, there is talk that Memorial Stadium will be razed. If that happens, the goose bumps certainly will rise again – only this time they will stay much longer. If it does happen, I predict a crowd of 40,000 plus will attend her final hour.

Clad in Gabardine knickers, Paul Baker enters Memorial Stadium with his dad for the 1944 Army-Navy game.
Photo: PB's private collection.

Paul Baker watches an Oriole game, in the 1975, while his sons enjoy one of their early Love Child experiences. Photo: PB's private collection.

WONDER YEARS
WWII *from the Eyes of a Child*

"Uncle Sam in a red, white & blue suit was always pointing a finger at us, and he looked pretty mean."

It was a cold and gray Sunday afternoon and we were playing dodge ball in the street when my father's voice suddenly summoned me into the house.

The Jap's just bombed Pearl Harbor.

I was almost seven years old and remember as if it were yesterday. December 7th will always be a day of reflection. For the nation and the world it was the beginning of an historic upheaval. For me, it signaled the start of my youth.

Almost overnight I developed a global awareness. TV was non-existent, but newspapers, radio broadcasts and *Life Magazine* were constants in our household. Dad was thirty-two – too old for the draft. My uncle Marion was eighteen and joined the Coast Guard.

My grandfather, who was born on the "other side" in Italy, lived with us. Every night we listened to the War news. Dad was a patriotic guy who admired Roosevelt, while Grandpop still held an allegiance to "Il Duce," whom I soon found out was Mussolini, the Italian dictator. Grandmom cried for all the Italian soldiers stranded in Ethiopia and

13

Mom worked in a tailor shop making Army uniforms.

After school I would listen to old radio serials like Terry and the Pirates, Jack Armstrong, and The Shadow. The radio was our source of entertainment, drama and news from the outside world. At night it was the ominous voices – Gabriel Heater, H.V. Kaltenborn, Walter Winchell and others – who had us riveted to the voice box. And of course, every so often we would hear President Roosevelt and British Prime Minister Winston Churchill give speeches on some really important stuff. I hung on their words and received a comprehensive geography lesson, learning the whereabouts of Leyte, Guam, Wake Island, Corregidor, Luzon, and Okinawa in the Pacific; Morocco, El Alamein, Tripoli, Libya and the Sahara in Africa; and Cherbourg, Bastogne, Normandy, Stalingrad, and Potsdam in Europe.

Names like Patton, Montgomery, Clark, Basilone, Goering, Rommel, Eisenhower, MacArthur, Nimitz, and Truman gave me a sense of drama and history. My career as a history teacher can be traced back to the news-reels, papers, magazines and radio reports of the forties.

As time went by I began to notice changes.

My dad became an Air Raid Warden and every week our neighborhood had to run an air raid drill. For one hour after dark we would pull down the shades, turn the lights down very low, and click off the radios. The Air Raid Wardens walked around the neighborhood with flash lights checking every house. When the siren went off it was a signal to resume our normal lives. We had to be ready if the Japs or Germans would bomb us. It was a very real feeling.

Throughout the community small flags appeared in the windows of some houses. The flag had a red border with a blue star inside a white background. Mom told me it meant the family had a person serving in the Armed Forces. If the flag had a gold star it indicated the serviceman had died.

Seeing the flags really brought the War home.

When the War started I was too young to go into stores alone, but I began to realize that candy and other good stuff was becoming scarce. Rationing started in earnest. Grandmom showed me the ration books every month. These books had pictures of meat, bags of sugar, and gas pumps. In order to buy these products, each family had to give up their allotted stamps plus the money. Fresh meat was a sometimes thing and a canned meat product, Spam, became a war time staple.

There were lots of ads in newspapers and on the sides of buses about buying War Bonds. Uncle Sam in a red, white and blue suit was always pointing a finger at us, and he looked pretty mean. Downtown on the corner of Baltimore and Charles Streets stood the Sunpapers building. From high up on the second floor came an electronic teletype with letters several feet high blurting out up to the minute news into the darkened streets below. Standing on that corner waiting for the bus, reading news from around the world was heady stuff. People would cheer or quietly mutter.

By 1944 I had become a fanatical sports fan and participant. The pictures in the papers and magazines had magnetized the psyche of a young child. And, for the first time I saw DiMaggio, Williams, Greenberg, Baugh, and Joe Louis on film in the MovieTone news, along with the unforgettable monotone of Lowell Thomas. On the home front, the Major Leagues were filled with old men, 4Fer's and young kids. The product was watered down. I listened to the 1944 World Series between the St. Louis Cardinals and the St. Louis Browns, who ten years later would become the Baltimore Orioles. In 1945 it was the exciting series between the Detroit Tigers and the Chicago Cubs. I can still remember the starting lineups. Here in Baltimore, the 1944 Orioles won the International League title then beat the Louisville Colonels in the Little World Series. Over 50,000 viewed the final game in Baltimore.

The War also changed the college scene drastically. To avoid the common draft, college players opted for Officer's Training in the nation's V-12 programs. Thus the service academies corralled the nation's best players. The 1944 Army team won the National Title, going undefeated and beating Notre Dame 48-0. They repeated in 1945 and again routed the Irish 59-0. After the war in 1946 they played to a 0-0 tie in Yankee Stadium.

In 1944, Dad took me to Baltimore Stadium to see the Army-Navy game. It was a bitter cold Saturday as the Midshipmen and Corps of Cadets marched down 33rd Street and into the wooden horseshoe that was Baltimore Stadium. The game admittance required the purchase of a U.S. War Bond and tickets were impossible to come by. Dad knew a fellow railroad man who was working a far gate, and in we went. Army had Blanchard and Davis, Mr. Inside and Mr. Outside. Both went on to win the Heisman Trophy. Navy also had a raft of stars led by Clyde "Smackover" Scott from Smackover, Arkansas. In a tough game, Navy died hard – 23-7. Fifty-three years and thousands of sporting events later, the thrill of the 1944 Army-Navy game remains fixed in my memory.

The War news was getting better and better. Adults were upbeat. The end was near. The corner grocery began to carry "candy bars." I had never seen a candy bar. All I ever got was "penny candy," sold loose for one and two cents a piece. Because of the ration system, candy bars were sent abroad to our troops, but all of a sudden in 1945, a little kid bought a Milky Way Bar and an ice cold Coke for a dime. Grandpop got a new car, Dad and Mom started going out to "night clubs" and Grandmom stopped crying over the boys in Ethiopia. The war was ending and we were winning.

On VJ (Victory over Japan) Day I stayed up all night and roller skated around the neighborhood as people celebrated on their front porches and car horns honked incessantly into the wee hours.

Four years prior, when my father called me into the house I was a child. By VJ Day in 1945, I had become a young man. The War Years absorbed me and filled my senses with hundreds of experiences.

What a classroom. These were my "Wonder Years."

My father's photograph of Navy's Midshipmen Brigade during the "March-On" at Baltimore (now Memorial) Stadium prior to the 1944 Army-Navy game in Baltimore.
Photo: PB's private collection.

SATURDAY'S HERO
Sandlot Football Memories

*"On Saturdays the fields were open and the little
squirts got a chance to cavort on a real football field."*

Back in the days before Pop Warner leagues and televised
football, we played the game for the sheer love of it. Sports
news was sparse and role models were hard to come by.
Magazines and newspapers fueled our imaginations and,
from 1944 thru 1946, I had amassed a collection of over one-
thousand football pictures cut out of local and out-of-town
newspapers.

The action game photos, with superimposed dotted lines
to show the path of the run or flight of the ball, were our only
"instant replays." At the theatre, MovieTone newsreels gave
us a quick moment of Slingin' Sammy Baugh of the
Washington Redskins or the explosive power running of
Army's Heisman Trophy winner, Doc Blanchard. Once, in
1952, we sat for more than four hours in the Irvington
Theatre just to see the newsreel of Billy Vessels' electrifying
touchdown run against Notre Dame for a second time.

Following the game closely, I would always come up with
a Saturday's Hero to emulate. In the fall of 1947 it was Emil
"Red" Sitko of Notre Dame. Also called "Six Yard Sitko", he

19

was a short, red-headed, powerful burst runner who led the Irish in yards gained for four consecutive years.

Early that Fall, a memorable Saturday was to take place for me. Despite having seen the Army-Navy game at Memorial Stadium in 1944 and having season tickets for the new pro team in town called the Colts, today would be my most memorable football day yet. It was an experience that would change my young life. It involved a redhead, but his name was not Sitko.

I began this day by playing less than a quarter in a 9 a.m. grammar school game at Slentz Field for the St. Joseph's Monastery School team, for whom I was a twelve year old seventh grade sub. Following this contest I tied my jersey, pads, helmet and shoes into a crude knapsack, wrapped it around the handlebars of my bike and set off on a four-mile journey to the noted Bloomingdale Oval and a neighborhood game arranged by one of our gang, Jimmy Foit, who was a high school freshman. He organized a game of tackle with a classmate, one of those "our neighborhood against your neighborhood" games.

As I arrived at Hilton Parkway, I could see Bloomingdale Oval (recently renamed for baseball Hall of Fame Inductee Leon Day) in the valley below. It was a municipal park where they had three full-sized football fields with goal posts, chalk lines and end zone flags – the whole thing. On Sundays, large crowds lined the sidelines of all the fields and vendors worked their way through the connecting gridirons selling refreshments. In the crowd you often heard play-by-play of a Redskins' game, but there were no tele-vised games in those days. These games were played with spirit and emotion and every community had its own team and colors.

On Saturdays the fields were open and little squirts got a chance to cavort on a real football field. I looked forward to the Saturday games, knowing there would be a chance for me to play. On my neighborhood team, I was a whirling dervish scatback. I could always get open and Jimmy could throw the ball close to fifty yards. The local tackle games with older guys also gave me a taste of the real action.

On my bike, I literally flew down the hill with my heart pounding from the ride and the anticipation. It was time for the kickoff.

Neither team had uniforms and everyone was dressed in his best football regalia. What a rabble! Dungarees were popular, along with hand-me-down wool jerseys replete with moth holes, sweat shirts, baggy canvas football pants with leather knee patches, and for the fortunate, helmets. Face masks were more than a decade away, and designer team jerseys were a quarter of a century down the road. We looked like the cast from an "Our Gang Comedy" film. My friend Franny Batz wore oversized olive drab canvas football pants with sewn in padding. These Jim Thorpe era pantaloons were held up by a blue Cub Scout belt with a gold buckle, and were set off with knee-high argyle socks. He topped it off with a subdued gray sweat shirt and a plastic tank helmet purchased at an Army surplus store. He was a big sixth grader slated for heavy duty line play, but on this day he was to be heard from.

As the two teams lined up, Jimmy and his classmate went over the rules. There were no adults and no referees, just a bunch of kids from two neighborhoods who wanted to play football.

Just before the kickoff, the clear Fall day was interrupted by a roaring noise, mixed with cheers from our opponents' side. Rumbling down the sidelines on a big red Cushman motor bike was their "champion," a wiry freckle faced redhead with a tattoo on his bicep and a pack of cigarettes rolled up in the sleeve of his T-shirt. He quickly dressed for action, puffing away on his cigarette, all the while giving orders to his subjects. What was really a motor scooter seemed like a Harley Davidson hog to us, and he appeared to be every bit of 25. He was actually 16 and mean, and at least two years older than any of us, but no one was about to question his eligibility.

The mood had shifted. No longer an even game, we were up against a "ringer", A ringer who cursed, smoked, rode a motorcycle, and had a real tattoo. As he looked us over with total disdain, a feeling of intimidation pervaded the air.

Our fears were well founded. Early on, "Red Bird," as we called him, ran circles around us. And, when we managed to tackle him, he came up punching and kicking. His teammates also got cuffed around for missing blocks or tackles. Playing in fear, we stuck together and gang tackled him whenever possible. After Red Bird ran through our entire team for a score, Jimmy wound up and heaved a long pass which I grabbed in full stride to tie the game. My great moment was cut short by Red Bird's arrival in the end zone. He flung me to the ground then threatened to bash my head if it happened again.

At the half we were tied 6-6. It was a warm day and we were all thirsty; however, no one ventured over to the water fountain where Red Bird had sequestered his troops. Several of our guys had bloody lips and swollen eyes, compliments of Red Bird, who chain smoked the whole game, mostly on defense. We vowed not to quit on each other and to finish the game no matter what. Bob Taylor urged us on, saying, "Don't let this bastard scare us, keep on his ass." As the second half began, we played with renewed determination. Red Bird's knuckle sandwiches became old hat, and we began to gang-tackle him harder. Franny Batz was on the bottom of every pile, and he was the first guy Red Bird would try to maul. He took some hard shots.

Late in the game, Jimmy faded back and let go one of his long bombs. Just like in the streets when I would follow the ball in its arc through the telephone wires, I kept my eyes glued to the ball as my tiny legs ran swiftly under it. Hauling in the touchdown pass, I looked over my shoulder for Red Bird. He was 30-yards away, too tired to ruin the moment. All the smoking and gang tackling had taken their toll. We prevailed 12-6. After loading up at the water fountain, some of our guys even had the nerve to holler catcalls in the direction of the redheaded bully who was mounting his chariot.

It was now nearly 2 o'clock and, just as planned, I would be home in time for the radio broadcast of the Notre Dame-Iowa game featuring a more benevolent redhead, Emil "Six-Yard" Sitko. But, before you could say CHEER, CHEER FOR OLD NOTRE DAME, Red Bird appeared out of nowhere on his big red machine. As our bicycle convoy made its way across the parkway to our neighborhood, he taunted us and challenged anyone to fight him. There were no takers. His motor scooter would veer into our paths, forcing us off the curb and into the street. With a cigarette dangling from his mouth, he looked pretty tough – and seeing that tattoo up close didn't help matters much. Somehow we weren't feeling much like winners. The tension was building and something had to give.

Suddenly, without warning, Red Bird flew off his bike and landed on his rear end in the street, the shiny red Cushman aimlessly spinning wheels on its side. Franny Batz had pushed over the bike, then slammed his Army surplus helmet to the pavement and stood menacingly over the bully. With a frenzied gleam in his eyes, Franny proceeded to pummel the bully into submission before our very eyes. It took only a few fleeting seconds and, when Franny, with clenched fists and flaring nostrils, asked the bloodied red head if he wanted more, there was no reply. A clean and decisive TKO.

In the meantime, we completed the revenge by pushing the Cushman down a steep embankment. The villain was suddenly left battered by the side of the road, with no transportation and no recourse. Justice had prevailed.

It was after two when we arrived home. I turned on the radio and Sitko had already scored the first touchdown. I was happy, but something seemed different. The Notre Dame game didn't seem so all consuming anymore. I had just completed my own "rite of passage", and there, sitting before me in the kitchen, eating a braunschweiger sandwich while holding a chilled bottle of grape soda to his swollen eyelid, was none other than Francis Xavier Batz – the real Saturday's Hero. As he smiled through a fat lip, we were both oblivious to the dramatic voice of Joe Boland. Franny never even knew who the hell Six-yard Sitko was anyway. And at that moment, I too, could not have cared less.

Five years later we were teammates on our high school football team. I heard that Red Bird became a cop. I still prefer to listen to Notre Dame games on the radio, and through the years, I occasionally wonder what Franny Batz is doing on Saturday afternoons.

THE CHALLENGE
Little Leaguer Faces The Bonus Baby

"I told him that if I had his talent I would be in the majors, and not sitting under a tree chugging a warm beer."

In 1948 I played CYO baseball for my parish team. Playing second base I couldn't catch a cold, but I could hit a little. I had my own bat – a $2.95 white ash generic Louisville Slugger with a fat barrel and a skinny handle. I shaved off all the varnish and the printing with an exacto blade, then taped the handle for a better feel. It was like having my own pool cue. Every time I got a hit I would gouge out a notch and fill it in with shoe polish.

During the summer I was cutting a swath through the West Baltimore 12-14 CYO League and my bat was peppered with notches. Walking home through the Mt. St. Joe campus I encountered Big Al Neville. He was laying out in his convertible under a shady tree sipping a brew. Al was a great athlete, maybe the best ever in our neighborhood. He was All-Maryland in baseball and basketball and he could kick a football out of sight. He had just graduated from high school and was a long and lean 6'-3", 175-pounds. Al and Dick Carr were the stars of St. Joe's MSA Champions. Both pitched and played the outfield. Carr was signed by the Yankees and did very well at Triple-A Kansas City before being brought up to the bigs by Casey Stengel in the 50's. Many believed that Al, who was 6-0 on the mound for St. Joe during his senior year, was in Carr's class.

On this day, for a lack of anything better to do, Big Al beckoned me over with the promise of a swig of his National Boh. He became fascinated with the shaved bat and the notches. When I told him the history of the bat, he started to convulse with laughter and his big Adam's Apple was jumping up and down like a Yo-Yo. He refused to give me a swig and would not return my bat. The exchange between the 8th grade Little Leaguer and the potential "Bonus Baby" began to get heated. He laughed at my "hitting prowess," all the while holding me at arms length from my precious bat.

I told him that if I had his talent I would be in the majors and not sitting under a tree swigging a warm beer. This statement hit a nerve and Al straightened up. One word led to another and I finally blurted out, "Give me ten swings and I'll base-hit your ass right now." Al's laid back demeanor changed. His eyes narrowed and he cursed at me, but he did return my beloved bat and headed for the mound. Long and lean, he had Jim Palmer's style (even though Pancakes was only three at the time), a big kick, long motion, and heat.

No one else was there. We set our own ground rules. I would get ten swings and would have to produce one base hit. We had three baseballs. There were no balls and strikes and no catcher. Al was clad only in a tight pair of shorts with loose canvas high-top Converse shoes. I was still in my wooly CYO uniform. As Al whistled a few fastballs over the plate, they crashed against the wooden backstop with resounding force. I began to get a little nervous and by the time I stepped into the batter's box I was shaking.

Batting helmets were still on somebody's drawing board. Al took a long swig on his beer, stared me down and

This is me, posing at Slentz Field, in my CYO uniform around the time of "The Challenge. Photo: PB's private collection.

unleashed a blazer that I missed late, by a mile. I rusty gated the next four, then finally fouled one off, giving myself a jolt of confidence. Beginning to relax, I let the next six pitches go by. Sweating, Al began to curse again, and called time out to fetch another beer. I fouled another one back and then hit a bouncer back to the mound which made him flinch and spill his beer. On the tenth strike I connected. It was a lazy loop-er into right field (my specialty) which I immediately deemed a Texas Leaguer. Characteristically, Al just laughed and called it an easy pop out. But the tension had broken along with my bat on the "basehit." We parted still bitching at each other.

When I got to the top of the campus hill and turned onto Frederick Avenue, the sounds of the traffic and people brought me back to reality. Looking at my cracked bat I began to tremble and broke into a cold sweat. I could have been killed back there. It's a good thing Big Al didn't throw at me. (That's probably why he never made the majors, but he did spend some time in minor league baseball.)

Years later Al ran a highly successful sporting goods store and his son, Al Neville Jr., broke several passing records at the University of Maryland as its star QB in the 70's.

THE LAST HURRAH

A Teenager's Farewell to Baseball

"This wasn't a game with a winner or a loser,
just a try-out camp in the middle of nowhere."

By the time I was 16 my baseball days were coming to an end. There were so many good players all over the City in those days. There were multi-diamonds at Patterson, Clifton, Herring Run, Carroll and Bloomingdale. In the 40's and 50's Baltimore sent hundreds of kids "away" to play pro ball in the Class D leagues. Al Kaline went straight from high school to the Major Leagues.

Throughout the City there were several high profile leagues for kids aged 14 through 18. The teams were city-wide in scope, a big cut above your neighborhood or CYO teams. If you made one of these squads, you became very visible. Your name would get into the books in which Major League scouts write. Many kids on these teams would receive minor league contracts.

In the Spring of 1951 I made one of those squads, Paul's Jewelry out of East Baltimore. We had great uniforms, just like the Philadelphia Phillies Whiz Kids, only in blue. I started the year at shortstop and was stinging the ball. But, I had trouble making all the plays and, when I made an error in the

10th inning that cost us a game against Gordon's Stores (Kaline's team), my days were numbered. I left Paul's in June and began to play pick-up hoops.

At this time there was a tiny kid in our neighborhood who was coming on like gangbusters. No more than 5'-4", 140-pounds, Joseph "Otts" Cascino was a whirlwind. He possessed power and tremendous speed. I would never consider racing him. One day in August, Otts calls up and invites me to go up to Elkton, Maryland with him to a Pittsburgh Pirates try-out camp. I reluctantly agreed. We got on the Big Dog downtown and several hours later were deposited in an open field in Elkton, Maryland – the shotgun wedding capitol of the nation and the Eastern Regional headquarters of the Klu Klux Klan.

It was blazing hot and there were well over a hundred kids on hand. We noticed dozens of Baltimore's best sandlotters there in the wings. These were just the guys from whom I was trying to distance myself. We went through infield and were timed in the forty. Everyone got a number pinned on their back, like in a cross-country race. I was #187. Otts and I got separated and they put me on third base with my weak sidewinder arm. The heat was unbearable and the drinking fountain was mobbed. I was mad as hell for listening to Otts, spending all that money on the bus ticket and getting no lunch.

When I finally got up to the plate late in the day, I was still pissed off and determined to make this damn day count for something. A tall fastballer with a high kick was on the mound, but I had seen Ralph Branca up close and personal and faced Al Neville in the flesh. I lined a basehit to center on the first pitch. Rounding first I heard Otts call out my name from the faceless throng on the sideline. I was all jacked-up and on the first pitch I took off and reached second in a cloud of dust. Everyone was coughing. This was an

Joseph Arthur "Otts" Cascino receiving The Lou Gehrig MVP Trophy from Mrs. Lou Gehrig at the 1953 Hearst Papers All Star Game, played in New York's Polo Grounds. Cascino led the USA All Stars to a victory over the New York All Stars.
Photo: Courtesy of McKeldin Library/University of Maryland College Park – News Post/News American

31

ugly, dry skinned diamond in the middle of a Maryland August. On the next pitch I flew into third with a pop-up slide and more dust. My entire body was covered with dirt. Now, everybody in the compound was watching and I knew it. The high kicker went into a stretch and looked over. I averted my eyes and stood motionless in a vortex of dust. He kicked and I took off like a banshee. Lucky for me the pitch was wild and in the dirt.

No one cheered. This wasn't a game with a winner or a loser, just a tryout camp in the middle of nowhere. But there was a murmur and a buzz of excitement as I trotted out to third. The Pirate scouts had gathered on the mound checking their clipboards. "Hey, number 187, what's your name kid?" They ordered me to throw some over to first. After a few throws, my sidewinder, second base arm began to betray me. The harder I threw, the more the ball tailed off. I knew it was curtains when Rex Bowen, the head scout, said, "O.K. kid, now cut it loose."

Needless to say, I wasn't called back. However, little Otts was. He went on to play with Leone's and Al Kaline. He became the MVP of the Hearst Papers All Star Game in the Polo Grounds in 1953 and spent several years in professional baseball in the Cubs' system. I never did play much baseball after that, but that shining, dusty moment still remains with me today. And whenever I drive past Elkton or hear a Pirate score, I think of that day long ago.

GROWING UP
The Summer of '51

"From that moment on I wanted to go to St. Joe and play on the football team."

Growing up on the west side of town in a large Catholic parish surrounded by cemeteries, there was an ethnic flavor to my neighborhood which was mostly filled with working class Irish Catholics and some Italians. The Protestants were descendants of indentured servants, and still struggling. Blocks upon blocks of row houses with scattered single homes and lots of trees gave the area a dimension and a personality. At night, the watering holes, pool rooms and bowling alleys, along neon lighted Frederick Avenue, were active outlets for the working stiff. It could pass for a Liverpool of past generations. We knew it as Irvington.

Further down the avenue was a prestigious Catholic high school run by the Xaverian Brothers. Mount Saint Joseph's was the last major stop on the Number 8 Trolley Line, a route that gerrymandered its way through the entire City of Baltimore. Transfer points placed kids from every Catholic parish grade school on the trolley track to St. Joe. The school became an ethnic melting pot. Every country in Eastern and Western Europe was represented at the Mount, seemingly on every trolley car. This natural network, plus the presence of a thirty-two team grade school basketball league run by the Xaverians, assured a flow of young athletes that made St. Joe an athletic powerhouse from the late 40's to the early 60's.

In 1947 I was a 5'-2", 105-pound seventh grader. Coming out of the Irvington Pharmacy, I heard a resounding echo coming from the St. Joe campus. I moved toward the sound and with every step it became louder. It was coming from a hollow deep within the tree lined campus and the loud cadence of a barking voice kept drawing me nearer.

Within a moment I was there. A thirteen year-old kid wearing corduroy knickers with a canvas book bag over his shoulder beheld an awesome sight – the Mt. St. Joseph's football team. Clad in clean white jerseys, khaki pants, leather helmets, and black high top shoes, they went through their paces with business-like precision. The chill of Autumn was in the air. The trees lining the practice field were turning brilliant colors. The scene held me spellbound.

Television had not yet intoxicated the senses and seeing the real thing for the first time was special. I had found my world. From that moment on I wanted to go to St. Joe and play on the football team. But, looking at those big guys on the field made my goal seem more like a dream.

In 1949 I was a freshman. The Mount went undefeated, winning the Maryland Scholastic Association title. They ran roughshod over nearly every opponent. Included was a 24-0 win over Patterson, ending their twenty-nine game winning streak. Located in the heart of East Baltimore they had become a football powerhouse for over a decade, even venturing into Pennsylvania with success. East Baltimore was the home of thousands of first and second generation immigrants. This victory was the high water mark for the ambitious Xaverians. Over 20,000 fans actually witnessed a neighborhood football game in Baltimore Stadium. Most of

Vic Wojcihovski was a "Rockne Era" blocking back for Notre Dame and our head football coach at Mt. St. Joe. Photo: Marge Wojcihovski Wood's private collection.

35

the St. Joe starters were also East Baltimore boys. Alumni of that game went on to play at Arizona, Bucknell, Kansas State, Richmond, Maryland, Virginia, VMI, and Wake Forest.

It is always tough to compare the playing calibre from decade to decade. But, the 1949 Mount team was the best that I have ever seen. They had two halfbacks who did not run the ball very often, yet in the Spring they ran the 100-yard dash for the track team in ten seconds flat.

Approaching the Summer of 1951 I was a rising junior and had grown to 5'6", 135-pounds. It was time to fulfill the dream.

Practice would start in mid-August. During the month of July I began to workout every night after work. In a field behind the local junior high school, P.S. #91, I would start jogging, then running, then sprinting. All the while faking, stopping and starting, spinning and changing direction against an imaginary opponent. When I got winded I would stop and catch my breath, then begin again in a burst of exhilaration. Over and over for close to an hour I would repeat the ritual. The workout would end up with sit-ups and more sprints. It was not sophisticated but it was great preparation. I was ready physically but still very nervous about the prospects.

On August 15, 1951 I rode my bike to St. Joe. Nearing the campus, dozens of rugged guys appeared. Off the street cars, in roadsters amid blaring 50's music, and on foot, they came. After one day, I left my bicycle home. It was the last vestige of childhood and now, I was in with the big boys – for better or for worse.

Our coach was Mr. Vic Wojcihovski, a Rockne era Notre Dame blocking back. He was raised in the coal regions of West Virginia and, outside of Mike Ditka, no NFL coach past or present compared to the menacing visage of Vic, who was silently called "Woj."

Wojcihovski came to St. Joe in 1946 as head coach for both football and basketball. He was born in Hungary before moving to West Virginia as a young child. He played at Notre Dame in the mid-30's, right after Rockne had established it as the greatest college football program in the nation. Vic was handsome, well dressed and worldly, as well as one tough, mean ass. On certain days, he wore combat boots to kick home his point, but mostly he brought pride and stature to St. Joe. He was the perfect role model for hundreds of ethnic kids from East Baltimore who made their way out to Irvington.

All sought his acceptance, some got his approval, and damn few received his praise. One who did, however, was Bobby Benzing – a boy off the #8 Trolley from Sacred Heart in Highlandtown who best typified the St. Joe spirit. Benzing was a spirited overachiever who played four varsity sports and, as a sophomore, was the spark of the 1949 football champs. As a senior, he was our inspiration. He was Vic's boy, the one exception from the fiery furnace, but none of us objected. Together, they were St. Joe football in this era and

TASTING A DREAM: *As a high school football player for Mt. St. Joe, in November of 1952, I (second from left, #23) got to play on the hallowed turf of Memorial* **Stadium.** Photo: PB's private collection.

37

to make this team would be very heady stuff.

Looking into Wojcihovski's eyes that first morning under a blistering August sun, surrounded by over one hundred candidates had me trembling with uncertainty. We went through thirty-minutes of boot camp style calisthenics. Twisting, rocking, reaching, bending and contorting into unimaginable positions. Then came the wind sprints – over and over in endless repetition. Guys started throwing up and fainting; they were dropping like soldiers on a Civil War battlefield. The weeding out process had begun. Hard work had prepared me. I was still standing.

The second day found me glued to my bed, seemingly paralyzed. Muscles refused to move. Every motion was met with stiff pain. The phone rang and my teammate Tom was in the same state. It took over ten minutes just to put on clothes. Somehow we made it to practice and only seventy-eight boys returned. I counted them.

After one week we were down to sixty and the nuances of real football began to appear. If you could remember the plays, follow your blockers, and take a hit without fumbling, then the odds began to tilt in your favor. The scrimmages and drills were rugged. We had no facemasks in the Summer of 1951. Bloody noses, cuts, and skinned up faces were common. There was no trainer on hand, only a few student managers with wet towels.

The Saturday before school started, when all of the young people were enjoying their last fling down the Ocean, we held our first live scrimmage – a dress rehearsal. This was the final test for the remaining sixty. The field was lined. The chains were out. I was in the third set of backs with my heart pounding and my knees shaking. "Remember the plays, don't go offside, don't fumble, run to daylight," I repeatedly reminded myself.

Stepping into the huddle, my number was called immediately – forty-seven counter on the two count. The rest was a blur in time. Two steps left, pivot into the hole and the ball was in my gut. I heard the smack of pads, some groans and realized, "I'm through." I cut right, spun off a linebacker and ran for the trees – all the way. The whistle blew the play dead and a collective applause of approval rose from the players. Without showing any emotion, I looked straight ahead, ran back toward the voices, and savored the moment.

That afternoon my dream had come true. Crouched in the huddle, barely sixteen, I finally felt part of something. A strong sense of accomplishment via hard work had become a valuable lesson. Walking past the Irvington Pharmacy and other Frederick Avenue landmarks now took on a different aura for me. I no longer rode that two wheel bike through Irvington – no St. Joe football player would do that. Life was now viewed through a different perspective.

In my own way, I was one with Wojcihovski, Benzing and all the great players who had come before. Sadly, Bobby and Vic both passed away in the Summer of 1996, just a few months apart, but I will always remember the time we shared and I will never relinquish my connection to them. Every kid should have their own Summer of 1951 on the way to the real world.

BEFORE TELEVISION
The Parish Church Hall

"I paid my 15 cents every Sunday night and was hooked for life.".

Every Catholic parish on the East Coast, coming out of World War II, had a church hall. It was a gathering place for the social side of life with God. All the pre-television diversions – bingo, card parties, suppers, oyster roasts, fashion shows, receptions, and of course, basketball – revolved around "the Hall."

We had such a place in Southwest Baltimore's St. Joseph's Monastery Parish. Located on the top floor of the school, it was a magical, magnetic place, called Whiteford Hall.

Once a month on Friday afternoons the nuns (School Sisters of Notre Dame) would march us upstairs, two-by-two, into the Hall. Even back then the slate steps were worn and beveled as they led us to an afternoon of enjoyment. Once there, we would view an old Harold Lloyd comedy or, if we were lucky, an Abbott and Costello flick. It always struck me that the nuns allowed us to laugh and carry-on during the movie, but never did they crack a smile.

In the fourth grade we would have a gym period up there once a week. It consisted of a 20 to a side rugby match with the ball, every now and then, going in the basket. It was my first exposure to basketball.

The Hall served many purposes. The basketball court was short, about 70-feet by 44-feet. There was a stage on one end, serving as the out of bounds line, with the backboard and pipes rigged flush up to it. At the other end, the basket was hung on the balcony edge that overlooked the Hall. So, it was fast break on the balcony end and perimeter play near the stage. On one sideline there was a bar – a bonafide tavern bar with taps, kegs, and a sink to serve the brews at parish functions. There was also another bar under the balcony and the Hall had an extremely high ceiling with lights hanging down like old lanterns. The place had a Gay Nineties, Prohibition like cast to it.

One night after an altar boys' meeting in one of the classrooms below, I wandered up the steps and there, in all its splendor and glory, was the Hall "at work." Coming up the stairs I heard the din of a huge garrulous crowd. Standing there in my corduroy knickers and plaid mackinaw, I beheld the Holy Name Society Oyster Roast in progress. Gambling wheels were turning to their clackety, clackety strain as wall to wall people were putting down their coins. Men were teetering around with pitchers of beer and fat cigars in their mouths. Raw oysters dipped into the deep-fry produced a "french fried" effect and thus oyster fritters. Other men slurped raw oysters down their throats between cold draughts. A little guy in an apron was selling raffle tickets. The parish priests were also there, mingling with parishioners and some Irish music was blaring in the background. By the time I was noticed, I had me two hot dogs and an oyster fritter.

The aroma of cooking meat, cigar smoke, spilled beer and raw oysters made its way up to the ceiling in a sort of "Holy Name Society" benediction, blessing the event. In the ensuing years it was no mystery to me why the Hall always had that stale smell.

Mostly, I remember some terrific basketball doubleheaders played there on Sunday nights by some unlikely looking guys, at least compared to today's standards. As a fifth grader, these were the first real basketball games I had seen.

The players were very serious and there was tension that you could see and feel. The several hundred fans who actually paid to get in, were on the edge of their chairs. The players passed the ball quickly with precision. Shots were only taken after much work and deliberation, usually with two hands. Players were bantering back and forth as they moved in their patterns.

I sat transfixed on the action until my trance was broken by the sound of a familiar voice. Standing in the backcourt, dribbling that laced pelota was Sonny Donahue, my baseball coach. Then I noticed the towel boy on the bench was Terry, who lived one street over. I envied him.

For the next few years, I paid my 15 cents on Sunday night and was hooked for life.

When TV came for everyone in the 50's, the traffic died down and a new era began. The disintegration of Colonial Catholicity had begun.

Section II

Sportsmen Who Came My Way

CHARLEY ECKMAN
Another View

"It is truly ironic that the great percentage of his followers never saw Charley ref a game. . . I saw both and he was better with a whistle in his mouth."

Back in the Summer of 1995 Charley Eckman passed away at the age of 73. He was a real, very visible personage who evoked a response from everyone. Those responses fell in three basic categories: love, hate or, the broadest of the three, reluctant affection.

Eckman was abrasive, arrogant, and very opinionated, with a minimal flip side to his gruffness. His word, to him, was gospel. He always argued and never lost. Intellectuals ignored him and educated folks poked fun. Charley's constituency was the common man – guys who liked to drink, gamble, and have a good time. He was the little man's gadfly, always poking fun at the establishment and often taking the unpopular stance. He handicapped horses with the best of them and, from his pulpit on the local airways, he put down every issue in the sporting world. He was a big advocate of the negative spin and he did it with his own inimitable style. With a gravelly, rat-a-tat, finger-pointing delivery of outrageous one liners, he was a combination of

Cagney and Ali.

But, more than anything else, Charley was an entertainer. People gravitated to the "machine gun" chatter. He fractured the English language and rattled your ear drums, but his stories are legend in Baltimore sports circles. Real celebrities avoided him as he craved their attention. Conversely, he made a living off of the slobs, whom he tolerated. His style did not permit him upward mobility. He was irreverent and crude – a Lenny Bruce in sporting mufti.

Eckman grew up in Baltimore during the Depression. A decent high school and sandlot athlete, he developed a tough style and exterior. He made his mark as a referee and umpire. Eckman and his emerging personality fed off the "power of officiating." During his heyday, he was better than the game – firing one liners, deflating egos, and banishing the unrepentant. He thrived on his "traveling vaudeville show," spitting out his own "Kangaroo Kourt" officiating justice.

He developed a great, confident style that was seldom questioned. All through his meteoric climb was Eckman's penchant for "making sure" the little guy got a fair shake. Officiating in sports has always been one-sided in favor of the home team and the favorite. During the 40's, 50's, and 60's, especially on the small college and minor league levels, it was practically impossible to get a fair shake on the road. Eckman, however, was a truly outstanding official who treated everyone fairly. He was a leader in the field of fair play and, as a referee, a viable candidate for the Basketball Hall of Fame.

Charley worked in all the top college venues up and down the East Coast, as well as throughout the country. Later he took his talents to the NBA and, in the mid-50's, Eckman, with his Cagney-like style, was actually hired to be the head coach of the Fort Wayne Pistons (now known as the Detroit

Pistons). He guided them to two NBA Division titles. Think of Ed Rush leading the Knicks into the NBA Finals or Ken Kaiser managing the Yankees in the Series.

Eventually, the Pistons, as Charley used to say, "made a change in his department." He never coached again, but the nickname "Coach" stuck with him for life. It is truly ironic that the great percentage of his followers never saw Charley

Charley Eckman was one of the greatest referees the game of basketball has ever known and a viable candidate for the Hall of Fame. (Note Eckman's City College ring on his left hand.) Photo: Courtesy of the Eckman family.

ref a game. They were hooked by his persona as a "character." I saw both, and in retrospect he was better with a whistle in his mouth.

In his later years, Charley hosted sports talk shows on a couple different local stations, did some commentary for the Baltimore Blast indoor soccer team, and served as an after dinner speaker. Today, Charley is missed, particularly by his family. With all the bluster, travel, and media hype, as well as the booze, tracks, and courts, Charley remained a family oriented guy to the end.

The bottom line on Eckman after all is scraped away, is "everybody gets a fair shake." He truly believed this and it was his credo. Much like Muhammad Ali, he brought sports out of the closet. He deserves to be enshrined forever. Truly a piece of Americana.

MUGGSY BOGUES
A Player

"He is completely fearless and no player playing today can force him to change his style."

Tyrone Bogues transferred to Dunbar from Southern High School and in 1983 he led the Poets to an undefeated season and the mythical high school National Championship, as voted by *USA Today* and other publications. The team was loaded with so many great players that their glow only made the tiny Bogues even more of a mystery.

Was he really that good? He couldn't be that quick, could he? Playing for and sparking this once in a lifetime team actually dimmed Muggsy's star. Very few major colleges were interested in him and the only looks he got were from schools who wanted Reggie Williams. Bogues made visits with Reggie and Wake Forest signed the tiny guard with Williams on the come. Georgetown, however, blessed Williams' grades, leaving the Deacons holding the Bogues.

I had seen Tyrone too many times to be fooled. I knew from the beginning that he would be a force wherever he went. At Wake Forest he became a national phenomenon as he proved to be among the finest point guards in the history of the ACC. Still, when it came to consider his chances for an NBA career, the nay sayers again came out of the woodwork. I stood by my original opinion and wrote the following analysis in the Spring of 1987, a few weeks before the NBA Draft.

Kenny Smith of North Carolina is probably the best guard in college hoops today. He will be on everyone's All-America Team and should be a first round NBA choice.

But, will he make it in the NBA? If so, will he last? What kind of career will he have? Is he strong enough to take the pounding? Will he be drafted by the right team?

When the answer is yes to all of these questions you have a sure fire pro. Despite all their expertise and experience, I doubt if most NBA Directors of Personnel can make anything more than an educated guess. The key in the case of Kenny Smith and any high draft pick is: "CAN HE DO THE SAME THINGS AGAINST PRO COMPETITION?"

At 5'-3", 140-pounds, Tyrone "Muggsy" Bogues is such a player. Tyrone "Muggsy" Bogues will play in the NBA. He will do his thing with a minimum of adjustment. Directors of NBA Personnel take heed:

- He dribbles the ball from <u>endline to endline</u> - <u>under control</u>, and <u>with a purpose</u>, quicker than any player I have observed in over forty years of close basketball observation.
- He cannot be pressed and no one can force him to pick up his dribble. He is a moving chess piece that dictates the pace and tempo of any game.
- He can do his thing against the Celtics, in a World Cup title game, in the ACC, and in an NBA Championship Series.
- His thing is: dribbling up the floor after a made or missed shot, full speed and under control, into the heart of whatever defense has gotten back, and then dishing off for easy chippies or wide open shots. A one man fast break who is constantly coming at you.

- For 8 to 12 minutes he could dominate the flow of any NBA game and make his teammates more effective. In the case of his present Wake Forest team that is young and limited, Muggsy's style only forces his mates into situations they normally cannot handle.

- He is an intimidator. A player who forces the opponent to change their game. Opponents are usually instructed to: 1. Get rid of the ball when he is guarding you; 2. Hold the ball over your head when he is in the area; 3. Try to take him low for a post up. On the other end it's, "get back quick," "loosen up and don't let him penetrate," and "pick up the open man." All of the above are reactions to a 5'-3" ball of fire. The opponents must adjust to him. In his own way Bogues intimidates.

- He is completely fearless and no player playing today can force him to change his style.

- He has super quick mongoose reactions and even the best ballhandlers are very wary of him.

Long before college and NBA scouts began to take Muggsy Bogues seriously, he was leading Baltimore Dunbar to mythical high school national championships.
Photo: PB's private collection.

- Defensively, Bogues makes his man do the following: 1. Pick up his dribble further out on the floor; 2. Pass the ball sooner than he wishes; 3. Turn his back in order to dribble; 4. Worry more about him than the game.
- Pound for pound Bogues is stronger than most college players and has been known to "tear" the ball out of the hands of larger players as he comes up unannounced from the blind side.
- If the ball is loose, it is usually his.
- All of these defensive traits are also constants, regardless of the level of competition.
- I have observed Spud Webb, Johnny Dawkins, and Pearl Washington (in a Five Star Summer Camp game) lose their composure when confronted head to head by Bogues.

The crowd will be behind him every night. They will be non-partisan where he is concerned. They will come out in droves just to see him. He is the perfect role model for the underdog. Tyrone Bogues will become a cult figure in any NBA city.

He is the consummate team player. He makes the other players better. He keeps the other players loose. He intimidates the opponents and makes them tight. He never stops hustling. He makes things happen. He is exciting. He is a performer as well as a competitor. He is a -- PLAYER.

Tyrone Bogues made me look like a prophet as he exceeded even my wildest expectations. Currently, he is in his 11th NBA season. He developed into a solid shooter and an excellent foul shooter. His assist to turnover ratio is one of the best in the history of the NBA.

Muggsy Bogues has opened up the possibilities for the little guy. Because of him, the NBA now has an open mind.

AL KALINE
Hall of Famer

"Here was an 18-year old who could swing like DiMaggio, throw like Carl Furillo and run like a deer."

Note: This story originally appeared as an Op-Ed column, submitted to the Baltimore Sun on December 23, 1994.

Al Kaline grew up in South Baltimore in a neighborhood called Westport, near Pig Town. The stockyards bordered Carroll Park, Al's home field. His roots were humble. Nick Kaline, a broom maker by trade never missed his son's games.

In 1953 at the age of eighteen, just a week after graduating from Southern High School, Kaline left his provincial roots, never to return. He went straight to the Detroit Tigers.

As a rookie he played some. The second year he started in right field and batted .276. The third year, not yet 21, he won the American League batting title with a .340 average. He never spent a day in the minor leagues. After that it was full speed ahead to the Hall of Fame. He was inducted in 1980.

Kaline spent his entire career with the Tigers, raised a family and became a successful business man. He never returned. He was gone before Baltimore ever got its American League franchise and became a lost soul in our firmament of sports idols. The Colts and Orioles clouded our sensory perceptions and gave us imported heroes who still live in this town today. It was like Al Kaline never happened.

But growing up as a peer, without the invasiveness of the tube, I remember Al Kaline well. Lanky, about 6'-2", he looked taller. He had a thin, craggy face with high cheek bones and a large nose. From day one he looked like what he was, a big leaguer. He ran with a loping gait, kind of loosy goosy, but when he rounded first base under a head of steam, his speed became apparent. His arms were lean and sinewy. He weighed no more than 170-pounds. His stroke was long and quick through the hitting area, not unlike Joe DiMaggio. Kaline hit line shots that carried over frozen outfielders, and through gaps into playgrounds and parking lots.   He attacked the ball regardless of who was pitching – high school stars or semi-pro vets. During the summers of his high school days he played practically every day against strong competition. This was to be his minor league experience.

Scouts came out in droves to see him. They would gather behind the wire mesh backstops of Carroll Park, Herring Run, Clifton Park, Bloomingdale Oval, and Spring Grove just to name a few. Out came the folding chairs, the stop watches, clip boards, and stoic glares. Never before, nor since, had any Baltimore kid drawn such attention. They would come early to see him throw. From center-field Al would charge the ball on a dead run, and in one quick motion come over the top, throwing perfect strikes to every base. The *coup de gras* were Kaline's throws to home plate. When he fired it on a line with no hops, Dick Lent, an outstanding receiver, would catch the 200-foot fastballs with a grimace and a puff of dust from his mitt. When Al threw the conventional one hopper, poor Dick could only grope for the ball like a beaten hockey goalie, as the ball pounded against the backstop.

Baltimore's greatest baseball treasure since Babe Ruth, Al Kaline went right from Southern High School to the Detroit Tigers, never to return again.
Photo: Courtesy of McKeldin Library/University of Maryland College Park – News Post/News American

My clearest memories are from the Mt. St. Joe-Southern game in the Spring of 1953 at Carroll Park. Kaline drilled a vicious one hop cannon shot to our shortstop who fielded it cleanly and quickly zipped it to first. Kaline tied the throw. In the same game with Kaline at third, he broke for home on a shot deep in the hole. The shortstop made the play and threw home. Our catcher, a football fullback, blocked the plate. Kaline came hard, spikes first, to a thunderous collision. Our guy held the ball. Coming off the field elated, we became quickly silent. Transfixed on our catcher's shin guards, we saw two puncture marks from Kaline's cleats. He had legs like steel springs. He was the first white guy I saw dunk a basketball.

Here was an 18-year old kid who swung like DiMaggio, threw like Carl Furillo, and ran like a deer. Our greatest baseball treasure since Babe Ruth, and he was about to leave forever.

These were just a few remembrances of Al and his greatness. Through the years I have heard many Kaline stories from his local peers. Remarkably, Kaline's style, carriage and accomplishments mirror those of another classy area player, Cal Ripken, Jr. Their batting records are quite similar and despite a divergence in playing position, they possess great throwing arms and are Gold Glove winners at their positions. Both have played with style and grace, never critical of teammates or rivals.

Al Kaline was with us for such a short time before he left to make his mark in the world. A fleeting talent, never again to be duplicated. He stands frozen in time.

In June of 1953, one week after we both graduated from high school, I watched Kaline as a Tiger in Griffith Stadium. He was not one bit out of place. He left us never to return.

Now, when I drive by an overgrown, usually empty Carroll Park, I think of Al Kaline.

HOWIE & BILLY
Their Memories Live On

". . .every B.U. athlete from those three decades would have their own favorite Howie or Billy story."

During the 50's, 60's and 70's Baltimore University had two of the most unusual and unforgettable athletic trainers to ever grace a college athletic department. Howie Pyle and Bill Ford were beyond Damon Runyon. Downright crazy, hard drinking oldtimers, they were actually well suited for the B.U. athletes, who were usually local kids from humble backgrounds, pursuing their only chance for a college degree and a better life.

B.U. had an open enrollment policy and a moderate price tag. Add in a partial athletic scholarship and a part-time job, and these kids made out O.K. But, juggling in practice, games, and partying made for some strange situations. Howie and Billy not only administered to the injured, they handled meal money, travel schedules, student work assignments, and homespun counseling on a wide range of subjects, including girlfriends, money, and priorities. In their own way they were perfect for the job.

Howie "Doc" Pyle sported a short, Roman emperor haircut with a dab of orange peroxide on the front edge. He had a glass eye that gave off a permanent gleam. He always wore his "dress whites" to every game and carried a black leather bag. A victim of Polio, Doc walked with a pronounced limp, but he was thick and physically strong, and a vociferous screamer on the bench. He sort of reminded me of Kirk Douglas as Doc Holliday in "Gunfight at the O.K. Corral" or Ragnar, the one eyed Viking in "The Vikings."

On road trips, Howie would board the bus carrying all of his trainer's paraphernalia along with two large tape cans. I wondered why we needed all that tape for just one game until it finally dawned on me – each tape canister held six National Bohemian Premium cans, previously iced in Howie's training room fridge. By game time he was ripe for action. For most of the B.U. athletes, especially the lacrosse and wrestling guys, he was a drinking buddy and confidant.

Despite his drinking and carousing, Pyle was an outstanding trainer in his, or any other era. He could tape an entire team in minutes, a "Picasso of the J&J." He dispensed advice with a bedside manner that relaxed the players and he was extremely cool under pressure.

In the Winter of 1961 I was the Assistant Basketball Coach at B.U. One night, our Captain Billy Frantz took an elbow so hard to the top of the head, that it opened an ugly, jagged cut. Blood was shooting out like a geyser. No sooner than we could put a towel on the cut, the towel would turn completely red. We carried Billy down to Doc's training room, bleeding, and I was in a clammy panic. Then Howie went to work. Donning rubber gloves with that glass eyed gleam, he assured Billy that everything would be O.K. His demeanor was calm and relaxed, like he was on a bar stool romancing a hooker (which hours later, he would probably be doing). Quickly, he shaved off the hair around the cut, pinched the jagged edges, and with his free hand began to stick a needle filled with novocaine around Billy's head as if it were a pin

Howie "Doc" Pyle, in the middle 50's, was an excellent, fun loving, hard living ath-letic trainer for Baltimore University, who will always be remembered as someone who gave more than he took. Photo: Courtesy of the Baltimore University archives.

cushion. Laughing and joking while ordering me around as if I were his scrub nurse, Doc sewed up the wound with pre-cision and neatly bandaged up the area. During the process I nearly fainted. As a precaution, we took Billy to the Emergency Room at Sinai Hospital. The doctor there took his vitals, admired the great work of "your team physician" and pronounced Billy sound. He played in the second half.

Earlier in his career Howie performed another minor miracle when the team bus ran off the road early in the morn-ing coming back from a lacrosse game at West Point. As the story goes, B.U. guys were strewn all over the highway, moaning and groaning. Howie, who was well insulated, leaped into action as he administered to every injured player on the run. He actually sewed up one guy's torn ear. When the police and ambulances arrived, everyone was resting safe and sound.

Despite his beloved stature around the B.U. athletic pro-gram, Doc lived his life in the fast lane. In my early years as the B.U. basketball and baseball coach, I met some sexy women early in the morning as they emerged from Howie's "training room" to shower and freshen up. He was a carousing, hell raiser who wouldn't have lasted 10-minutes in the modern, politically correct world of college sports. And, even though most of his antics were overlooked, it was Howie's "wild side," which eventually caught up with him.

One night during a heated B.U.-Towson hoop game, Towson's Dave Possinger and our Stanley Zunt were going at it all game long. Fisticuffs seemed imminent, as I repeatedly implored Stanley to remain cool. However, late in the game Possinger inflamed Stanley with a body block. Jumping to his feet, Stanley raced up court with revenge and rage in his eyes. As he passed our bench, I threw myself into his path, hoping to restrain him before he could maim Possinger. His churning knees collided with my head and neck as we tumbled to the floor. Everything went blank for a few seconds and, as I came to, I realized a full-fledged brawl was underway. Looking up I saw veteran official Frank Matecki trying to restore order, but before I could scramble to my feet and offer some assistance, he was suddenly blindsided by a roundhouse right. A mouse the size of a golf ball formed instantly over his eye and, standing over him was a crazed, seething Howie Pyle.

Frank Matecki was always a controlled, even tempered official and I never understood Howie's motivation. Evidently, he had been harboring a grudge against Matecki for some time and he took this opportunity to express his feelings. The next day Baltimore University ended Howie's career. No matter how much he was loved, he was not going to survive this. Paul Menton, the Sports Editor of the Sunpapers, as well as the Commissioner of Officials and a trustee of Baltimore University at this time, wanted his head and that was that.

In light of the circumstances, Howie's dismissal was warranted. But, it must be said that Howie Pyle gave more than he ever took from B.U. The players loved him and he remains a vivid memory of days gone by.

Following Pyle at the helm of the B.U. training room was Billy Ford, another piece of work. Ford started out as the Baltimore Bullets' ball boy before moving on to equipment manager. Eventually he began to wrap ankles. He took some course and, magically, he became a trainer overnight. While with the Bullets, Ford instigated a bench clearing brawl involving his beloved Buddy Jeannette and referee Norm Drucker, but he is more fondly remembered for his mouth-to-mouth resuscitation of the famed referee Mindy Rudolph who had collapsed at Madison Square Garden.

When B.U. sacked Pyle, Billy jumped right into the opening because it was a full-time position with benefits and he had a young family. He was not the trainer that Howie was, but the burly, overly gregarious Ford threw his weight around our Mt. Washington campus for nearly a decade. His size and demeanor were likened to the famous pro wrestler Gorilla Monsoon. He became the buffer between coaches, athletes, and administrators. Taking the side of the "most aggrieved," he was always in the middle of something. All the while he was learning how to be a trainer.

People who interacted with Billy ran the gamut of human emotions with exasperation being a constant. He was also the type of guy that you couldn't stay mad at for very long. Billy was a former cab driver and bartender. He understood and accepted the urchins who came off the streets to try on a college education. A former Forest Park athlete and sandlot footballer, he was one of them – a cantankerous bumpy ride – but like the proverbial mother hen, he was always there when most needed.

Although Billy was not known as the partier that Howie Pyle was, he still drew some attention after hours, as my long time assistant Jim "Snuffy" Smith remembers.

"Billy Ford once tried to long jump from the main bar to the service bar at the Wishing Well Lounge at three a.m. one morning. He came up short and got up and left without knowing that his leg was broken. Ralph Boston could not have made that jump in his prime," said Snuffy. "Billy could double for Humphrey Pennyworth. He was a big teddy bear, party animal and cab driver. Trainers are a different breed and Billy was the last of a species."

My most memorable recollection of Billy Ford's career concerns a snowy trip to Erie, Pennsylvania to play Gannon College. After a rough flight we landed in snowbound Erie. Our party of 18 was set up in three station wagons. The highways were snow covered and a fine sleet was pelting our windshields. With a wrinkled map on his lap, Billy announced that he knew the exact directions to our hotel. With that he roared out of the airport with the other two wagons in pursuit. Ford, who was a dead ringer for the late actor John Candy, seemed to ignore all the signs and intersections. Finally he spotted a "landmark," jammed on the breaks and made a left turn, only after we completed a beautiful 360-degree pirouette. Hellbent on getting to the hotel he ignored pleas to slow down. As he righted the wagon and hit the pedal, I saw a sign saying, "Welcome to Presque Isle State Park." After a mile we began to see ocean going vessels moored out in the distance on both sides. It was apparent we were on a peninsula and we sure as hell weren't headed for downtown Erie.

Another mile and the visibility was getting worse. The ships became ghost like shadows. In the distance, out on the frozen lake, was a lone hunched up figure, sitting on a box, ice fishing. Ford again jammed on the breaks, bolted out of the wagon and began to scream out his dilemma to the shocked fisherman. Before Ford could get any directions

Big and burly, Billy Ford, who followed Howie Pyle as B.U. trainer, threw his weight around the school's Mt. Washington campus.
Photo: Courtesy of the Baltimore University archives.

there were two distinct thuds about five seconds apart. Station wagons two and three had rear ended the caravan. Ford's wagon had gotten a double shot and we had a three car pile up in a snow storm in the middle of nowhere. If Billy had stopped a little farther up, all three vehicles might have made it over land's end into Lake Erie, which was only a few hundred feet away. Miraculously no one was badly injured, although one guy had a severely split lip. Where was Doc Pyle when you needed him? Picture yourself as the Ice Fisherman that day.

Ironically, it was another auto accident that led Billy Ford to meet his Maker, prematurely, in a 1972 head on collision in the Harbor Tunnel. He left this world on that day, but not before leaving a lasting impression on hundreds of B.U. athletes. I would venture to say that just about every B.U. athlete from those three decades would have their own favorite Howie or Billy story. Their memories live on.

DICK PAPARO
A Night at The Opera

". . .rather than poetry in motion, he is an Italian opera."

In the old days when men were called referees instead of officials, for better or worse, fans knew them by name. They were more identifiable, more human. There was no hiding in anonymity. These throw back guys were a big part of the game's growth and flavor. Lou Bello, Charley Eckman, Red Mihalik, Steve Honzo and, more recently, Hank Nichols represented the old guard.

With the advent of the three-man crew in 1980, basketball officiating came of age. The speed, size, and athleticism of the modern player cried out for this change. Three men now divide the floor and systematically administer the game. They are anonymous and, for the most part, efficient.

Officiating major college basketball means big bucks. The top conferences pay their officials well over $500 per game. The modern big time official has a profile. He is an athletic, slender, well organized, politically correct, college educated professional. His median age gets younger each year and minorities are well represented.

In the midst of this hi-tech profile is an old fashioned referee who does not fit the afore mentioned mold. He is a remnant of days gone by. He is Dick Paparo out of Syracuse, New York. Nicknamed "Froggy" for his *basso profundo* voice, he breaks all of the stereotypes. Paparo does not have a college degree, does not have a flat stomach, and does not possess a classic style. And now, at the pinnacle of his career, he labors to carry his weight.

At 6'-1" and around 215-pounds, he looks like the catcher he was back in the 60's, when he had his cup of coffee with the Chicago Cubs. After a game he relaxes with vino, spaghetti, espresso and cigarettes. His speech patterns include deep whispers, loud pronouncements, and poetic license with the King's English. The stories mixed with his unique delivery are pure Damon Runyon laced with Mario Puzo. He talks like he refs, with a unique flavor and gusto.

Froggy is universally respected by coaches and players alike. He is constantly requested by teams playing in big intersectional road games. Coaches have the utmost confidence in his judgement and fairness. He is the guy you want to see on the road. Players relax with his earthy style. They feel a human bond – from his voice, persona, and body language. His strong, on the money calls, cut tension and put the game back on track.

Paparo is perceptive and street smart. He is the veteran traffic cop, the all knowing bartender, the drill sergeant. Yet, he knows the rule book better than his new wave mates. It is his bible, the cornerstone for his confidence and style. At the officials' seminars, he asks the insightful questions.

It is sometimes difficult for the new wave guys to work with Froggy. He fractures the symmetry of the three man crew by asserting his style on the game, all over the floor. It could be said that he still refs in the two man system and, sometimes, he can be accused of working alone. Paparo's style is macho assertive. Rather than poetry in motion he is an Italian Opera. If a fellow official is tentative, he will drown in Froggy's wake. If an official is strong, Froggy makes room. He leads and challenges his partners to join him. When the game pressure is at its hottest, he is at his best. He never fades out.

Dick Paparo is the last of a breed. The three man system has put his kind out of business. The flat bellies are here to stay. In the meantime, coaches and players will continue to respect his efforts and play worry free.

BUDDY JEANNETTE
Player, Coach, Hall of Famer

"I can still see, frozen in time, the haze of cigar smoke framing Buddy's two-hand, underhanded layup."

Note: **This story originally appeared as an Op-Ed column, submitted to the Baltimore Sun on January 20, 1995.**

Tonight at the Baltimore Arena, the Washington Bullets will honor Harry "Buddy" Jeannette. They used to be called the Baltimore Bullets and, in 1948, won the old NBA Championship. Buddy was the inspirational player-coach of that squad. This past Spring he was inducted into the Basketball Hall of Fame in Springfield, Massachusetts.

The game has changed so much since Jeannette's days. It seems a lifetime ago. He was just a decade removed from the center jump after each basket. There was no shot clock, no dunking, no three point line, no black players, and no television. Games were played in dingy, smoke filled arenas and one of the prototypes was our own Baltimore Coliseum on Monroe Street. Still standing today, it was a square warehouse-like structure with a movie marquee posted out front. The Coliseum hosted wrestling, boxing, roller derby, public roller skating, and in the 50's, rock and roll concerts. The place was dusty, ugly, and aged even then. The locker rooms were tiny and nails served as clothes hangers. It had a hard scrabble persona all its own, right out of an old James Cagney movie.

On game nights, the place would come alive with enchanting sounds of electric organ music (which is still used in the NBA today) and the cooking smell of the all beef hot dogs (which don't have that aroma today) permeating the air. On Saturday nights I would hop a ride over from my West Baltimore neighborhood and spend a total of $3.50 for a ticket, a hot dog, and a coke each half. We would always pick up a stray program in the corners of the building where older men in heavy overcoats would be puffing on thick stogies, street talking, and behaving nefariously. Their blue language and the thick cigar smoke rose to the rafters, settled, then wafted over the court in a sort of pregame benediction. The court was brightly lit, framed by the complete darkness of the surrounding bleachers. The courtside seats were arranged on risers with the rows and chairs designated by chalk markings that rubbed off on people's clothing. It was not a place to go dressed up. The boards of the court would rumble, squeak or groan, according to the traffic of each fast break. Mice and rats lived in the building and cats were set loose after games to regulate the cycle of life.

It was in this setting that a 13 year-old boy learned about the game he came to love, and to see some of the greatest basketball players in the world. In addition to Buddy Jeannette I saw seventeen other players who performed in the Coliseum on their way to the Basketball Hall of Fame. They were Paul Arizin, Al Cervi, Bob Cousy, Bob Davies, Joe Fulks, Harry Gallatin, Bob Houbregs, Neil Johnston, Ed Macauley, Slater Martin, Dick McGuire, George Mikan, Andy Phillip, Jim Pollard, Dolph Schayes, Bill Sharman, and Bobby Wanzer.

Buddy, in his era (1938-48) was a truly great player and

Even as a young college player, Buddy Jeannette had the look of a star. He went on to become a leader among men and found his way into the Basketball Hall of Fame. Photo: Courtesy of the Basketball Hall of Fame, Springfield, MA.

leader of men – a rare combination. Standing a little under six feet and weighing around 175 pounds, he had long arms and big hands. He was a premier ballhandler. Not fancy like young Cousy, he threw precision two-hand chest passes. His passing set the team in motion. They were Buddy's X's and O's. He was a strong driver who set his man up off picks and screens. He also possessed a soft shooting touch from the outside. His trademark was the two-hand, underhand foul shot. Harvey Kasoff, a retired local businessman who was the Bullets' ball boy recalls, "Buddy was my idol. When he stepped to the foul line and took that deep breath, everybody in the Coliseum breathed with him. He was money in the bank from the foul line in the closing minutes."

Paul "The Bear" Hoffman was the NBA Rookie of the Year with the Bullets in 1947-48 and he has made his home in Baltimore ever since. He recalls, "I have never seen a player win more games for his team in the final two minutes than Buddy. He would always find a way. Setting up the offense, driving to the hoop, stealing the ball, making foul shots. We always felt we could win with Buddy on the floor."

Robert "Jake" Embry, the Bullets' owner who also had a piece of the Colts, made Buddy the highest paid NBA player of his day ($15,000 annually) and compared him with another two minute miracle man. "Buddy was the greatest competitor I've ever seen. He is an inspirational leader and he had great determination to find a way to win. The only other athlete I would compare him with was Johnny Unitas," stated Embry.

Jeannette never averaged much more than ten points per game. But point totals were much lower then. He was a winner everywhere he went. As one of basketball's early pioneers he played on five championship teams in four different cities. Buddy was revered here, but with the advent of modern basketball, his Hall of Fame bid kept coming up short.

The Baltimore connection kept lobbying for his induction. Harvey Kasoff, the old ball boy, led the charge. Ex-*Sun* Sports Editor Seymour Smith, who was the Bullet beat writer back then, along with sportswriters Alan Goldstein, John Steadman, and Bill Tanton, kept the flame alive. Jeannette's college roommate at Washington & Jefferson, Kenny Mason, lobbied for years from his position with Eastman Kodak. His induction last May was a greatly deserved triumph of the spirit. These people would not let the legend die. It was only fitting that Buddy got in "in the closing minutes."

The high point of his career came in Baltimore in the 1947-48 season when the Baltimore Bullets beat the New York Knicks in the Eastern Semi-Finals, then finished off the Philadelphia Warriors for the old NBA title. The Knicks were the league's premier team. Owned and operated by the great Madison Square Garden promoter and entrepreneur Ned Irish, they played to huge crowds of over 15,000 even in those days. Irish and his entourage came down by train to the Monroe Street Coliseum to see their boys whip the upstart Bullet team before going on to face the Warriors for the title. Comparing Madison Square Garden to the Monroe Street Coliseum was like Marilyn Monroe measuring up with Marjorie Main. But we had Buddy.

In the closing seconds New York's Carl Braun, who had this high dribbling style, was slowly burning time off the clock, protecting a one point lead. All of sudden Buddy lunged across Braun's elongated frame and with those quick hands got a piece of the ball, caught up with it and drove in for the winning basket. I can still see, frozen in time, the haze of cigar smoke framing Buddy's two-hand, underhanded layup. The place exploded. Ned and his big city boys got back on the train pronto. Baltimore got on the map by beating Philly for the title. Later, our 1958 Colts and Weaver's Orioles gave New York our calling card, but it was Buddy and his feisty Bullets, from the Monroe Street Coliseum, that first put this town into the big leagues.

Had he lived in another era Buddy Jeannette would have been a household name. In the championship series with Philadelphia, the team was 20 down when Jeannette tore the locker room door off its hinges. Somehow they rallied to win. He had the competitive drive that all the great ones have. And for this he remains a player for all eras.

This night for Buddy Jeannette forms a closure of sorts for both he and the Bullets. Buddy will be 78 in September. Truly a living legend, he resides with his wife Bonnie in Nashua, New Hampshire. The Bullets will be moving further into Washington with the construction of a $200 million arena in downtown Washington, DC and there is talk that they may change their name. The new arena is scheduled to open for the 1997-98 season, fifty years after the Bullets' first world title in 1948. Time marches on and seldom looks back.

But tonight in the Baltimore Arena, when Buddy Jeannette is honored, clap a little harder. You are not just looking down on an old man. You are looking at a guy who had the fire of a Bobby Knight and the competitive spirit of a Michael Jordan. I felt it a privilege to know him and to have seen him play. With all my experiences of over four decades in basketball, Buddy Jeannette and his accomplishments still rank at the top. Quality transcends time.

Buddy Jeannette recently turned 80 and still attends the Hall of Fame Dinners each year. Harvey Kasoff calls him regularly. The Washington Bullets changed their name to the Washington Wizards prior to the 1997-98 season.

VINCE DUNDEE
My Compare'

"Around 1924 Vince met Paulie Mugavero at the Grand Theatre in Highlandtown. Young teenagers, they became fast friends."

Vincent Lazzara was not a super talent in his era, or any other. Standing about five-feet, nine inches at 150-pounds, he was not very muscular. In fact he had a lean and gangly look. He was not the hard-nosed, tough guy you associated with professional fighters, and he had no punch to speak of. Rarely did he ever knock out an opponent. And, he certainly didn't have that killer instinct. The prototype fighters of his era were the downtrodden and depraved of a hopeless society. Brutish men lacking in conscience and soul. Vincent Lazzara was not of that genre.

He came up big in natural instincts. Clever, he avoided punches. He was quick and long armed. Vince was confident, intelligent, and mentally tough. Boxing fans loved him. If you went to the fights, you would end up rooting for Vince. He was Mr. Everyman of the Depression, fighting the pugs of hopelessness. Vince was an ordinary guy working in a ring to survive in the game of life. He succeeded just enough to stay ensnared in the trap. A trap that would contribute to his premature demise.

In the 1920's literally hundreds of young Italian immigrants and sons of immigrants attempted to establish their manhood by stepping into the boxing ring. Fighting in social clubs around the city by night and working in menial hard scrabble jobs during the day they led a precarious existence.

This is a story of one of those young men who fought his way out of Baltimore's "Little Italy" to become Champion of the World. Vincent Lazzara's career started during the Roaring Twenties and finished at the end of the Great Depression. Spanning two decades between the World Wars, these periods ran the gamut of human emotions. During the 20's the nation flaunted itself against all the social mores of the past. It was the era of the Jazz Singer, the Charleston, the Black Bottom and Prohibition. For the first time people broke loose and were judged as individuals. Station in life took a back seat. Just one decade later, the Great Depression pushed the Roaring Twenties out the back door to the sobering effects of joblessness and despair. Vincent Lazzara's life was to mirror these eras with haunting clarity.

Born in Palermo, Sicily in 1908 he was the youngest of four brothers. The family settled in the Belair Market section, on the edge of Little Italy. His father ran a fruit stand. Vince and his brothers worked the stand and ran the streets. The older brothers fought as amateurs and Joe Lazzara became very successful. Despite a long and lanky frame it was only natural that Vince would follow his lead.

Around 1924 Vince met Paulie Mugavero at the Grand Theater in Highlandtown. Young teenagers, they became fast friends. Paulie worked in a pool room that turned into a dance hall by night. They hustled girls, drank hooch, shared their money, and their hopes and dreams. Both got into the ring. Vince was a natural. Quick and agile, he seldom took a hard shot. Between 1924 and 1927 Vince won 40 consecu-

Vince Dundee stood only 5'-9" and packed very little muscle onto his 150-pound frame, but he was quick and agile. Photo: Paul Baker's private collection.

tive amateur bouts. Brother Joe had turned pro. It fueled the younger Lazzara's dreams. The brothers changed their name to Dundee after a family of famous Scottish boxers. Vince developed a local following with his crowd pleasing style.

In the meantime Joe Dundee was closing in on the welterweight title. On June 3, 1927 in front of 22,000 in New York's Polo Grounds, Joe Dundee won the title from Pete Latzo of Scranton, Pennsylvania. (It was also in 1927 that the New York Yankees, arguably, had the greatest baseball team of all time, the Dempsey-Tunney famous long count bout took place, and Lindbergh made his Trans-Atlantic flight. It was a Golden Age.) In the midst of the Roaring Twenties Baltimore went bonkers. Front page headlines and a downtown parade heralded the event. Joe became a local legend, and for that era, a wealthy man. He kept the title for two years before losing it to Jackie Fields on July 25, 1929 in Detroit, on a disputed foul decision.

At the age of nineteen Vince Dundee turned pro. Fighting in local clubs in and around the area, plus a series of successes in the Newark, New Jersey area, Vince amassed another string of 40 straight victories. Leaving the club scene Vince followed brother Joe out to California. For a kid from Little Italy in the 1920's, it was a gutsy move. It was to be his proving ground. Because of Joe, Vince got matches and moved up fast. He was, as they say in the business, a crowd pleaser. Never taking a backward step, bobbing, weaving, and slipping punches, he delivered a lightning quick body attack. Vince's stock in trade was his pure boxing instincts. "He can ride punches. He can make a blow miss him by the fraction of an inch. He is especially clever on the ropes," said Los Angeles Times boxing scribe Sol Plex in 1928.

Out west Vince was having the time of his life. Yet he was lonely and uncertain. He wrote Paulie at every turn. On one hand he loved the Hollywood lifestyle, the girls, the parties, the fast lane. There were occasional trips to Tiajuana between fights and always new experiences for an East Coast ghetto kid to savor. He bought clothes he had only dreamed about and even purchased a car. The scene out there was the precursor of the modern day muscle beach lifestyle. "All the women out here sure like boxers." And it never rained in California. Paulie got the clippings, the stories, the scoop and always the plea for news from home. After every fight, Paulie got a telegram with the decision and a request to "go over the house and tell Momma I'm O.K.," and always the reminder to keep writing.

In the ring he was making quite a name. George Raft, Jack Dempsey, Jess Willard, plus various and sundry young movie stars where his pals. He sent Paulie boxing magazines, oranges, plus shirts and ties from the fashion boutiques. Paulie sent clippings, Baltimore newspapers, neighborhood news and encouragement. In 1929 Vince lost a split decision to Jackie Fields, a transplanted Chicago Jew (Jake Finklestein), who was also chasing a dream. At the time it

In California Vince's career began to flourish, but his ability to purchase luxuries such as new clothes and cars did not relieve the lonliness he experienced.
Photo: Paul Baker's private collection.

81

was considered the best prize fight ever staged in the State of California. Vince was barely 21. He and Fields would eventually become champions as Fields would dethrone Joe Dundee later that year. Vince would have a longer path. Making the 145 welterweight slot was getting harder. Vince was still growing. He would become a middleweight.

California began to run its course. Vince came home a man. He needed more polish and a program. Baltimore was still a club town. There was no money to be made there. And the Stock Market was about to crash. Despite his heroic title victory and euphoric home town greeting, Joe Dundee could never work up a title match in Baltimore. Vince knew his future was elsewhere. The great Jack Dempsey had now become a promoter, referee, and manager. Having seen Vince on the Coast, he had become a big booster. Dempsey put Vince in the hands of two crafty boxing people. Max Waxman became his manager and Benny Benjamin became his trainer. They had previously handled Joe Dundee and Dempsey himself. The triumvirate took-off. Several fights in Madison Square Garden made Vince one of the most popular boxers on the East Coast. Vince moved to Newark and his career was now on a collision course with fame. "Vince Dundee is acclaimed one of the most graceful and clever boxers in the ring. He has a magnetic personality and a happy go lucky disposition. He is a favorite because he is one of the crowd for whom he exhibits," said the Newark News in 1930.

The letters kept coming. The Depression was in full swing. Paulie was running the pool hall and looking for a better job. Vince remained upbeat. He met the girl of his dreams. His letters no longer had the hollow ring of loneliness. He had outgrown his Baltimore roots. All during this time of growth and strife, hundreds of Dundee's letters were written with a tone and grammar that belied his grade school education. Filled with hope and fear they mirrored a

In 1930, Vince moved to New Jersey and met the girl of his dreams, Connie Rossi. Soon they would marry and have a son. In less than three years, he would become a World Champion. Photo: Paul Baker's private collection.

moment in time, for both him and the era. Slang and profanity would have been out of place. There was none.

Vince married Connie Rossi in Belleville, New Jersey. Paulie Mugavero was the dashing best man. It was right about the time of the Stock Market crash, October 31, 1929. In 1931 Connie gave birth to Vincent Lazzara, Jr. and the family settled in Belleville. Their new home bore a striking resemblance to an earlier California post card of a famous movie star home that Vince had sent to Paulie. He had developed a champion's tastes.

Throughout his career Vince was always concerned about his livelihood. Purses were never large and expenses were high. Dundee made New Jersey his home turf. Waxman and Benjamin established tough training camps, put some meat on Vince's bones, and made him a stronger puncher. Max judiciously matched him against the proper opponents. Over the years Dundee would fight over 150 bouts, winning 112, losing only 18 with 14 draws, five no decisions and one no contest. During the Waxman regime Vince and Connie toured Europe. On July 10, 1931 he lost a split decision to Marcel Thil, the French champion in Paris. Vince wrote to Paulie, "I beat Thil up good, but couldn't knock him out. The decision was expected in a foreign country." The European trip served a purpose. It kept him on the title path. He would later decision Len Harvey twice in the same year. Harvey, the British champion is considered by many as the greatest fighter in the history of Great Britain.

Vince was always training. Always in the gym. Always running. He would average a fight a month for 12 years! And other than the typical boxer's pug nose he was relatively unscathed. A tribute to his boxing skills.

At the tender age of 25, Vince Dundee won the middleweight title. He defeated Lou Brouillard over 15 rounds in Lou's hometown of Boston, on October 30, 1933. The title was not unified at that time with Thil holding the European version. After 10 years of fighting the best in the world, Vince Dundee was the champion. Right in the middle of the Great Depression. Unlike brother Joe's tumultuous acclaim in 1927, Baltimore and the nation hardly blinked an eye.

Within the year Vince successfully defended his title against Andy Callahan in Boston and Al Diamond in Paterson, New Jersey. The purses were small by title fight standards and Vince still had a family, a mortgage, and expenses. Looking for the big payday in the middle of the Depression became an obsession. Finally the opportunity came calling. Teddy Yarosz, a young Pittsburgh tiger with a great hometown following who had beaten Vince a year earlier, was in search of the crown. They offered a $25,000 guarantee with no rematch clause. It didn't take Vince and Max long to agree. Vince was always supremely confident. Along with his innate skills it was his trump card. In his letters to Paulie were always references of his belief in himself. He had fought so many home town guys and still managed to

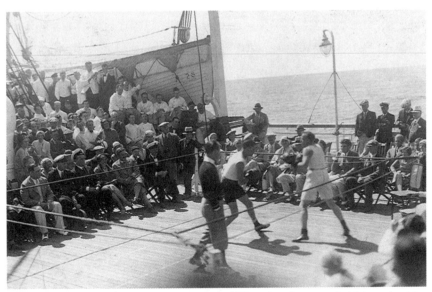

In 1931, Vince and Connie sailed to Paris and Vince fought several shipboard exhibitions as he prepared for a bout with French Champion Marcel Thil.
Photo: Paul Baker's private collection.

win. He won on his skills, his courage, and his ability to sway the fans and judges. His letters also hinted that boxing was really just a means to an end for him – a way out of poverty – a chance for the good life. Signing to fight tough Teddy Yarosz in his own hometown for a chance at the good life was a done deal for Vincent Lazzara of Little Italy. That pact had been made long ago.

On September 11, 1934 in front of 28,000 partisan fans in an open field in Pittsburgh, Vince Dundee and Teddy Yarosz fought a savage toe to toe battle. Yarosz won the title. Dundee walked with $25,000. By today's standards it equated to a $450,000 payday. In the midst of the Depression Vincent Lazzara did what he had to do. Still young and relatively unscathed, with no other marketable skills, he went back to the gym, as Waxman searched for some paydays.

During this time Vince wrote Paulie about a training camp injury. He had twisted his knee so badly that it swelled to an enormous size. When the swelling subsided, the pain began. "Paulie, every time I make a quick movement it feels like a knife is shooting through my knee." Several local bouts were canceled. But less than a month after the letter to Paulie, Waxman signed Vince up for a $3,500 payday against veteran Freddie Steele. They traveled by plane but the trip to Seattle took two days. On July 7, 1935 Dundee, who had never been knocked out in his career, was beaten so badly that the fight was stopped after three rounds. He had been knocked down eleven times, receiving a broken jaw and brain concussion. He was only 27. Even though Freddie Steele was an outstanding puncher and eventual champion, there was no plausible explanation as to why Dundee would receive such a beating. One can only surmise about the knee and what it did to his speed. The time lag from the long trip may have been a factor. Or, it could have been a cumulative affect. So many fights unscathed. He retired. He began to sign his letters Vincent Lazzara, as if to distance himself from a life that was really not his. In the Fall of 1935 he came back to Baltimore to be the *Compare* '(Godfather) to Paulie's son. He showed the affects of the Steele beating with slurred speech and a swollen jaw.

Washed up with no job and no prospects, he kept writing to Paulie. He refereed (in those days ex-champs were in demand to fill the house), opened a body and fender shop, and tried to get on the payroll as a police officer. In 1937 he actually fought again. Three bouts, winning two. His last big fight would ironically be in Pittsburgh. They brought the old war horse, all of 29, into town to face the greatest young fighter to ever come out of Pittsburgh. His name was Billy Conn. Conn who later grew into a heavyweight was a hot, undefeated (30-0), 19-year old middleweight on the rise. He would eventually fight Joe Louis twice for the heavyweight title. The first meeting was a boxing classic for all time with

In 1934, Vince (L) lost his World Middleweight Championship in a brutal 15-round battle, before 28,000 fans who gathered in an open Pittsburgh field, with young, hometown favorite Teddy Yarosz. Although he dropped the decision, Vince was paid $25,000 (the equivalent of $450,000 today) which helped him achieve his goal of financial security for his family. Post-Gazette Photo by S. Yarosz 1934: "Copyright, Pittsburgh Post Gazette, all rights reserved. Reprinted with permission."

Conn leading heavily on points before the Brown Bomber put him away in the 13th round. The fight took place in New York on June 18, 1941 before America went to war in earnest. But on this night Vince Dundee would call upon all his abilities and inner strength to give the young Irish whirlwind a lesson. Harry Keck of the *Pittsburgh Post Gazette* in his story of May 4, 1937 had this to say, "Two winners walked out of the ring after the main bout in Duquesne Garden last night. The official winner was Billy Conn, sensational 19-year old middleweight. His opponent, who lost the decision but won the crowd was Vince Dundee, ten years older, a former World Champion. Never within our memory has a loser received such an ovation." Billy Conn was quoted as saying, "Mr. Dundee, I learned more tonight than in all my other fights. I want to thank you for the lesson. You are the best I ever fought." Vince went out in style. And in his letter to Paulie he claimed, as he had many times before, that he should have gotten the nod.

In 1939 Vince and Connie miraculously escaped death in a violent auto accident at a railroad crossing in New Jersey. According to the January 23, 1939 edition of the *Baltimore News Post*, the car was hurled over 300-feet. Both received serious injuries and were hospitalized. There was a long rehabilitation period. Paulie visited and kept getting letters. Vince vowed to get through these hard times. Young Vince was doing well in private school. But the accident traumatized Vince.

By 1940 he began to feel the affects of his long, hard road. Ten years of constant training, travel, endless bouts, the Steele beating and then the accident began to tell. He came to Baltimore. I remember sitting on his lap. He was kind and gentle with a faraway look. His speech was slurred and his face was puffy. He was only 33. A modern day Muhammad Ali comes to mind as I recall that meeting of long ago.

Doctors diagnosed Vince's condition as Amyotrophic Lateral Sclerosis, a hardening of the spinal cord, causing the muscles to shrivel. It was the same disease that felled Lou Gehrig. There was no cure.

Later that year Vince and his family moved to California. Back to the scene of his early success. It was no longer the Roaring Twenties or the Depression. The New Deal of Franklin D. Roosevelt was underway. Paulie now had two jobs, working at the Pennsylvania Railroad ticket office and moonlighting in the Parimutual Department at the Maryland Race Tracks.

In one of this last letters Vince wrote Paulie with an offer to run his California bar and lounge. It was too late. Paulie had a family and found his own way out of poverty. Vince was retired to the Laurel Sanitarium in Glendale, California. It was 1942. He glided through World War II, his son's high school graduation and his wife's vigil. His son read him letters from Paulie and his many friends, right up til the end. On July 28, 1949 Vincent Lazzara passed away in his sleep. He was 41-years old.

He lived a short life. A fast paced trip through two of America's most tumultuous decades. He reached the pinnacle of his profession, married a beautiful loving woman. They produced a sweet boy child whom they loved dearly. Vince chased fame hard. It was fleeting and cruel. The fruits of his labor enabled the family to get a start in California. And there is a happy ending. Vince Jr. became an attorney and a very successful restaurateur and caterer in Southern California. He has four highly educated children and two grandchildren. Connie Rossi Lazzara is still alive and well living with her son at the age of 87. Paulie passed away in his sleep on January 11, 1995. He was 85. In his possession were hundreds of letters written to him by Vince during the 20's and 30's.

Vince Dundee fell through the cracks of time because of the era in which he lived. He also changed his name which cut him off from his Italian roots, and the pantheon of great Italian Champions. As a gentleman, he was compared to Gene Tunney. He was great with the press. He loved the spotlight. He enjoyed the moment. In his day there was limited media coverage. After the war our world expanded and heroes came popping out of the MovieTone Newsreels, AP photos, and television. He missed all that. In another time and place he would have been a media darling. Vince fought ten hard years to get his title shot – an unheard of odyssey in today's "it happened yesterday existence." During his brief moment in time, Vince was the best.

Vince is my *Compare'* and Paulie is my father.

DICKY KELLY
East Baltimore Legend

"Kelly flourished in the dingy gyms where every voice and sound was magnified and you could feel the crowd breathing down your back."

James "Dicky" Kelly was a basketball legend in the Baltimore inner city long before he got a college degree. I first saw him in 1964 as a Dunbar 10th grader. He stood out from a crew of highly talented school yard players. Perhaps it was his light skin, but more than that, it was his stop on a dime, poetry in motion jump shot.

In the middle 60's college recruiting was still primitive. There were no recruiting services and no talent camps. The prestigious Five Star Camp, where many future Dunbar stars were discovered, was non-existent. Kelly was the last of the great Dunbar players to go unnoticed. He went to Maryland State (now UMES), got homesick and was back in Baltimore before Christmas. Dicky got married, raised a daughter and began to play sandlot basketball. For five years he won every tournament MVP and broke every scoring record in town. The Spring tournaments used to bring together recent college grads and local semi-pros. Fans swarmed to these events. ESPN wasn't here yet. One night in Dundalk, Dicky hit ten straight jump shots from 20 plus. Whenever he got the ball, people would pause in hushed anticipation, and then erupt in spontaneous applause with every bucket.

Finally at the age of 25 Kelly decided to get educated. Along with some other street guys, he matriculated to Bay Community College down on Howard Street. A product of the State and Federal bureaucracy, Bay lasted less than ten years, but it gave Dicky a chance to start over. In 1973-74 he averaged 40.7 points per game to lead the national junior college scoring parade and got his A.A. degree.

At this time I was the coach at Wheeling College in Wheeling, West Virginia and, one night when Dicky was playing up in Pittsburgh, I took Henry Sutherland, our faculty advisor, and one of the Jesuit priests to see him. Dicky went for 50 plus, nailing jump shots from every angle. My companions were astounded and asked the inevitable question, "Could we get him to come to Wheeling College?" Surprisingly, the big schools again overlooked him, always searching for tall guys. Part of the problem was that Bay did not qualify for the JUCO Nationals, due to their new status, denying Dicky larger exposure. Thus, he fell through the cracks again and right into our open arms.

That summer he went to camp with the Philadelphia 76ers and almost made their roster. His eligibility still intact, he came on up to Wheeling. Throughout his two years with us, Dicky evoked the same reaction from crowds everywhere – hushed anticipation every time he touched the ball. Kelly was a straight up and down player; no shake and bake or dipsy doodle. His signature since puberty was speed, quickness, and touch. He had the uncanny ability to freeze the defender, and in an instant, release a picture perfect jump shot before it could be contested. His touch would adjust. The twenty footer was as soft as the pull-up jumper in the lane.

Dunbar legend James "Dicky" Kelly in 1965, the year he led the Poets to the MSA title with a championship game victory over City College.
Photo: Courtesy McKeldin Library/University of Maryland – Baltimore News Post/News American collection.

Kelly flourished in the dingy gyms where every voice and sound was magnified and you could feel the crowd breathing on your back. He had played his entire career in this environment. An old gunfighter or bare knuckle street fighter, you were glad to have him on your side.

Dicky was a hardened street guy who bore the scars and scrapes of his upbringing. He looked his age. And, on a Winter's night in 1976 while crossing the Canadian border, a heart stopping incident occurred.

We were making a week long, mid-semester trip up to Montreal, Canada for two games before heading to New Jersey to play Jersey City State and St. Peter's. During a driving snow storm our charter bus pulls into one of the border crossing stations. Onto the bus comes a Canadian Mounted Policeman with a drug sniffing German Shepherd. It was just a random check and, after going over the trip manifest with the driver, the Red Coat informs me that he must randomly select one of our passengers for a routine search. In a 46 passenger bus filled with players, cheerleaders, faculty members and coaches, he picks Kelly. As Dicky disappeared into the swirling snow I began to think negative thoughts; the dog tipped off the Mountie, the Mounties always get their man, and we may never see Dicky again. Visions of Turkish prisons danced through my head. If he was carrying anything with him, we were all dead meat. I began to think who our Congressmen were. I also envisioned the Mounties tearing through all our luggage in that driving storm. The bus held its collective breath as James "Dicky" Kelly, from the streets of East Baltimore was ushered into that holding pen. Fifteen minutes later he emerged and sprinted to the bus, sporting a wide cheshire like grin. We burst into unbridled cheers and laughter. Kelly was clean. We knew it all the time. The Royal Canadian Mounted Police couldn't lay a hand on the home boy.

Nearly 30 years old, Dicky Kelly graduated from Wheeling College in 1976 after two
brilliant seasons. Today, he remains "the only NBA calibre, Jesuit educated fireman
in captivity," as he works for the Baltimore City Fire Department.
Photo: Paul Baker's private collection.

In the Winter of 1976, as promised, I brought the team to Baltimore for Dicky's rather belated homecoming. He was 28 and about to graduate from a Jesuit college with a degree in Sociology. Towson State was a Division II power in the midst of a cluster of 20 plus win seasons. The game was played in dirty, dusty Burdick Hall on the TSU campus. It was Dicky's type of venue. There were about 1,500 seats on one side of the gym. On the other side of the court there was a giant divider partition. Dicky's whole neighborhood was there. Both newspapers covered the game and that "hushed anticipation" hung over the building like a growing summer night storm. Behind our bench was an amalgam of East Baltimore street blacks and Wheeling College honkeys – all united, all hopeful. As we were warming up, two of Dicky's buddies ran over to the partition and, with the help of some heavy duty duct tape, hung a bed sheet sign with a spray painted message in street vernacular, "GO DICKHEAD, SERVE TOWSON'S ASS."

No one said a word. For a moment, hushed anticipation gave way to dead silence, except for the two dudes who were crowing over their handiwork. I was biting my tongue holding back the laughter. The band broke the ice and everyone got back to rockin' and rollin. When the referees saw the sign they informed the Towson officials that the bed sheet must go. The question was, who was going to take it down. Towson wisely sent over an older black janitor. You could have cut the tension with a knife. He proceeded to remove the "banner" with care, folding it gently over his arm and walking off to a loud applause. Old Glory couldn't have gotten better treatment.

Finally, the game was on. It was tense and close all the way. Kelly played 25 minutes, scored 23 points on 9-of-14 shooting and put the game away with three consecutive buckets in the closing minutes for a 90-86 win. The sign proved to be the signature for the game. Dicky was surrounded by press and well wishers and his shots appeared on the 11 o'clock news. It was truly his night.

In his two years at Wheeling College our record was 47-19. He scored over 1,400 points, averaging right around 20 per game. He made first team All West Virginia Conference and Honorable Mention All American. And, despite his "advanced years" he seldom missed a practice. He worked hard and led by example. He treated his teammates with respect, from the starters to the lowest subs. In his last game, after a tough defeat, he broke the silence with a simple statement, "I really enjoyed playing with all you guys."

Millions of basketball fans are familiar with Baltimore's Dunbar High School. Her distinguished alumni numbers NBA standouts such as the late Reggie Lewis, Reggie Williams, Tyrone "Muggsy" Bogues, Sam Cassell, and David Wingate, as well as former college stars like Ernie Graham, Larry Gibson, and Keith Booth. Dicky was as good as any of them. His time was a little too early – had he been born ten years later he would have been in the NBA.

Today Dicky Kelly works for the Baltimore City Fire Department at the Gay Street Station – the only Jesuit degreed, NBA calibre firefighter in captivity. Even now, whenever his name is mentioned in conversation, a hush of anticipation fills the air as if he might appear out of thin air and sink another "J."

NICK SCHLOEDER
Gilman's Affirmative Action Hire

"Over the next 39 years it became apparent that a traitor was in their midst."

In the fall of 1955 after attending three high schools and Towson State, I found myself still floundering as a student at Baltimore Junior College – a step away from manual labor. I had wanted to be a coach and already had some experience with youth groups. But, a college degree and a path to a good life was fading fast. No one in my family ever had a chance to go to college, and despite my parents' support, I was slipping.

About this time I met Nick Schloeder. Just 25 and fresh out of the Army, he was a sight to behold. With his short blond brush cut and fierce demeanor, he made the Montebello Grade School gym come alive with tension. We were a rabble of untalented, underachieving nobodies – Nick's introduction to Baltimore.

Remembering our first game at powerhouse York Junior College, it was just like yesterday. There were 1,000 people packed in a tiny gym and I was nervous. But, in the first minute of play I cut the tension as my patented two-hand set shot rippled the cords. Seconds later I found myself on the bench as Schloeder barked, "run the offense and no outside shots."

99

This was the first of many confrontations/revelations between Nick and I. Only a few years apart in age, I could relate to him. Our away game bus trips, that invariably ended in losses, were education highlights for us because we got a few hours of hearing and being with "Nick."

After the first semester of more academic chaos, I was about to accept a job with the Paul J. Adams Paper Company. Nick talked me out of it (He couldn't afford to lose that set shot.). He boiled it down to the basics. "Which subjects do you enjoy most?" he asked. "Sociology," I replied. I also liked the teacher, Ms. Leona Morris. He spoke with her, got me signed up for just 12 credit hours. I got three B's and an A and never looked back.

In my coaching career I always tried to help kids the way he helped me. Therein lies one of Nick's legacies. But, after his days at BJC he went on to do even greater work, as he changed the outlook and philosophy of an entire institution.

Hopelessly mired in patrician elitism for over a half century, Gilman School, an Ivy prep school in Baltimore, was lurching and grinding to an ignominious crawl. Approaching Vietnam and the social upheavels to follow, the school was in great need of change.

Along came Nick Schloeder. Initially, he appeared to be "one of them." Bucknell educated via Peddie Prep, he had a scholar's bent and he could coach more than a few sports. The ideal prep school workaholic teacher. But, Gilman got more than it bargained for. Over the next 39 years it became apparent that a traitor was in their midst. He questioned everything and everyone. The old traditions were still sacred, but they were no longer gospel. In his classroom laboratory, on the playing fields, and in the board room, Nick questioned the status quo. Schloeder was at the center of so much controversy that former Headmaster and Gilman immortal Redmond C.S. Finney used to refer to himself as Nick's "defense attorney."

He was largely responsible for the great diversity that has now become the trademark of the new Gilman. As the school

Nick Schloeder helped straighten out the academic fortunes of a young Paul Baker at Baltimore Junior College, then went on to do the same for young men at Gilman School for more than 39 years. Photo: Courtesy of Nick Schloeder, Jr.

turns toward the 21st Century, its face is no longer craggy and pre-defined. Rather, it has a soft, wide, illuminated visage. Gilman is no longer just a blue blood Ivy prep domicile. Nick Schloeder did this. In a methodical, caring, questioning and probing manner, he turned the establishment inside out, making them see themselves, good and bad. Thus the winds of change gripped Gilman.

During his 39 years, Nick also helped many students on a personal level – guiding, focusing and encouraging – just as he had done for me so many years before. The school will forever be in his debt. We can all stop to reflect in our own lifetime on the teachers that touched us and turned us toward the light. Nick Schloeder did this for me. He also left and everlasting mark on Gilman and the many students he taught.

RAY MULLIS
The Colonel

"He yelled and screamed the entire game, brandishing a red towel which he alternated between waving and chewing, long before Tarkanian."

When a person is referred to as a "crazy son of a bitch," it can be an invective or a term of endearment. With Ray Mullis it went both ways. But I suspect, the better you got to know him, the more endearing he became. But Ray preferred the latter, obviously.

I first met this cantankerous individual during the 1964-65 season. Our Towson Catholic team was the class of the area going 26-4. That year we beat Cardinal Gibbons by 30 plus, emptying our bench early. Gibbons was in its first year of varsity basketball. There was no pressure on them to achieve that day, but their coach was taking an aggressive, combative stance. He yelled and screamed the entire game, brandishing a red towel which he alternated between waving and chewing, long before Tarkanian. After the game Mullis stormed into our coaches' room, and with a heavy Georgia twang, let us know in no uncertain terms that 95-60 was not going to happen in the future. He showed a lot of gall and my assistants dismissed his tirade, calling him among other things, "a crazy son of a bitch." I knew better. This guy meant business.

Thirty-one years and 620 wins later, Ray more than proved his point. He settled in, building a program that won lots of games and influenced young lives. And as his success mounted he did become just a trifle more subdued. His Crusaders appeared in twelve Alhambra Catholic Invitational Tournaments, more than any Baltimore Catholic League school. After the 1964-65 season I left Towson Catholic to coach on the collegiate level. Ray never got a shot to get even with me, a fact that he continually brought up whenever we were together.

Ray Mullis should not be characterized as just a great coach with over 600 wins and a fist full of titles. He was more than that. He was a stickler for certain things. His teams were disciplined. They played hard on defense. He instilled team and personal pride. They played with enthusiasm. Unlike most coaches, Ray knew the rule book, and woe to the official who came into his lair unprepared. He got on officials for 31 years. Still, his players always had a sense of fair play and respect for authority. Although he was a "crazy son of a bitch," he didn't tolerate craziness from his players.

Ray did all the things coaches have to do at Catholic Schools – driving vans, sweeping floors, washing uniforms, tutoring kids, locking doors, closing windows, adjusting thermostats – for 31 years. Ray moved in the day the school opened and when he walked into the new gymnasium, which had stands on only one side and a steep windowed wall on the other, with the Principal, Br. Matthew Betz, S.M., he commented, "Who was the #@*&#@$ idiot that designed this place?" To which Br. Matthew replied, "That #@*&#@$ idiot was me."

Ray's biggest contributions were in teaching. He was an excellent Algebra teacher and an incisive teacher of basketball fundamentals. I always felt honored to speak at his Summer camp. Then I began to realize that the real reason he invited me was to continue to remind me of how I escaped his revenge back in the 60's.

Ray Mullis was a winner, as his 620 career victories at Cardinal Gibbons clearly testifies. But, first and foremost he was a teacher. Above he drives home a defensive point at the McDonald's All Star Classic and in the two insets he works his magic at the famous Five Star Basketball Camp. In the top inset, future NBA star and "Dream Teamer" Alonzo Mourning (center) listens intently to the instructions of Coach Mullis and, in the bottom inset, my son Steve (dark T-Shirt), who is now an assistant coach at New York University and a long time instructor at Five Star, participates in a Mullis drill. Photos: Courtesy of Mrs. Mullis

Ray loved to smoke, drink, play cards and bet a few bucks here and there. The all night card games at the Alhambra were legendary. Some say that Ray drove his squad to success every year so they could get the Alhambra invitation, but this wasn't true because win or lose, Ray and his entourage would be shuffling 'em at the Alhambra anyway.

The past few decades Ray had graced the famous Five Star Basketball Camp with his presence and, despite the many more prominent faces there, he soon made his mark, on and off the courts. It was at Five Star in Pittsburgh where Ray got his late-in-life nickname. He and several Five Star coaches were refused entry into an after hours night club. Ray demanded to see the manager who turned out to be an inebriated thug with bulging biceps. The coaches stepped back. Ray stepped up. Noticing a USMC tattoo, Ray quickly concocted the story that he served in Vietnam and was indeed Lieutenant Calley's C.O. at Mai Lai. Somehow the guy bought the story and the Five Star guys were ushered into a first row table as the bouncer publicly introduced "Colonel" Mullis to the cheering throng of Pittsburgh drunks. Ray's gall had won the night. The word spread like wildfire the next day at camp and, from that day forward, Ray Mullis was "The Colonel" to all Five Star coaches and campers.

In February of 1988 I was in St. Joseph's Hospital recovering from a heart attack. Late at night the ICU Ward can be a scary place. Total darkness interspersed with green and red flashing lights and pinging noises. Through the eerie darkness I was waking from a deep sleep. In the corner amidst the bleeping machines, a shadow moved. Dressed in black it moved closer. I was gripped in fear. Was it the Grim Reaper? Had I bought the farm? My fear subsided as I saw the red and white Crusader letters come into focus and heard the Georgia twang. The Colonel had just stopped over to see how I was doing. It didn't matter that the roads were covered with snow that night. Ray had been in an out of hospitals himself so he was sensitive to my plight. I later told him that he just didn't want to see me depart without one more revenge story.

On December 17, 1994, Ray Mullis coached his final game at Cardinal Gibbons. His Crusaders beat Gilman for Ray's 620th win. Two days later his battle with pancreatic cancer ended. There had been time to celebrate this mans contributions. There was a 25th Anniversary party that rocked and rolled into the wee hours. In September of 1994 there was a Testimonial Dinner establishing a scholarship fund in his name. Ray left knowing how people felt about him. His last major college recruit is Steve Wojciechowski of Duke. An undersized over achiever, Wojo stresses teamwork, defense, and discipline. He embodies the spirit of Ray Mullis.

As Cardinal Gibbons struggles to remain a viable force in Baltimore Catholic education, they should remember the efforts of Ray Mullis.

FRED HIKEL

A Matter of Principle

"He didn't believe in make-up calls, the home court, or big reputations."

Fred Hikel came to Baltimore in the early 60's. He migrated from Clarksburg, West Virginia, seeking the good life as a gym teacher in Baltimore County. Along the way, to earn extra bucks, he refereed basketball games. He was good right from the start.

I first saw him work in a JV high school game. Fred had that innate ability to cut through the controversy. Nothing was a grey area for him. He made the calls and administered the game with a clear, concise style. Without calling attention to himself, he was nevertheless, a commanding presence. The ref was as good as the game.

Despite being an "immigrant without papers," his reputation spread quickly. He went from JV to varsity to college ball in the wink of an eye. Fred Hikel was a natural. He transcended the politics and petty favoritism that is prevalent in officiating. He shot to the top of the charts – a lone wolf on acapella solo.

In the early 70's he worked the top conferences on the East Coast. Hikel did the famous UCLA-NC State game in 1973, featuring David Thompson and Bill Walton. Prior to the advent of the three man crew and the TV explosion, basketball officials made peanuts. Even the big time conferences were poorly administered by aging bureaucrats who hated their jobs. During this period there was terrible officiating and, while the behind the scenes shenanigans were taking place, Fred Hikel stood out like a beacon in the night. He was beholding to none; no coach, no commissioner, and to no other officials. He got there on the sheer strength of his work ethic and innate ability. Although admired, he was resented. Fred never backed down from his convictions. He didn't believe in make-up calls, the home court, or big reputations. He called the game as it unfolded. No more and no less. The players were not weighted according to seniority, ability, or color. They were all the same.

When egocentric coaches could not get to him they bitched to commissioners. Usually the commissioner would approach Fred about diplomacy. It was fruitless. With Hikel it was a matter of principle.

In the early 70's he called a travel in the Baltimore Civic Center on a quick Dunbar High guard who had stolen the ball on his way to the winning layup. The noise was so deafening you couldn't hear. In the face of this screaming throng, he stuck to his guns and "brought the play back." Most refs would have ignored the travel. With Hikel it was a matter of principle.

In the late 70's at Georgetown, Big Sky Shelton of the Hoyas knocked the ball away from the rim on GW's Haviland Harper with no time on the clock and the score tied. Hikel made the goal tending call to give GW the win and John Thompson didn't say a word. Fred Hikel was a man of principle.

On March 6, 1975 at the ACC Tournament in Greensboro, North Carolina, Wake Forest was leading North Carolina 90-86 with 34 seconds to go. Wake threw a length of the court pass for the game clincher. Fred blew the whistle and ruled the ball had touched the bottom of the overhead scoreboard. The trajectory did not change. He caught a lot of heat when Wake lost in overtime. Fred Hikel fell victim to the political

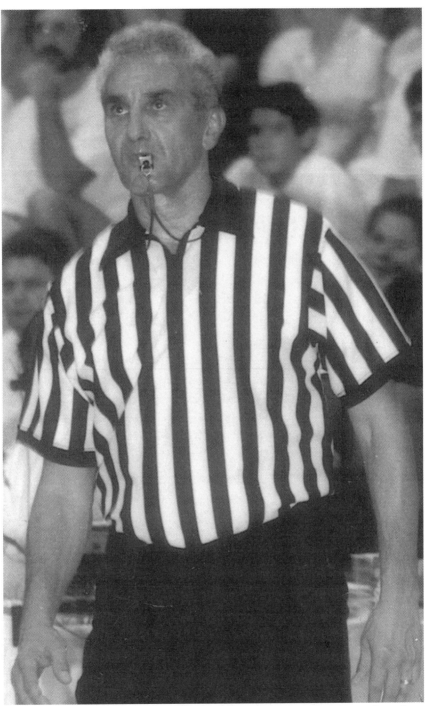

Fred Hikel overcame adversity and politics to make his mark as a top notch, major college basketball referee. Shown here working the 1992 Maui Invitational Tournament in Hawaii. Photo: Fred Hikel's private collection.

system.

Shortly thereafter, Fred Hikel's life was to change forever. While serving as a traffic monitor at his junior high school, he was blindsided by a speeding van and thrown 100-feet in the air. He was on life support systems for weeks. Fortunately there was no brain damage or spinal problems. Everything else was broken, but not his will.

Months and months of painful therapy kept him out of his teaching job and basketball.

In two years, Fred Hikel came back. By this time the old boy system was ending, being replaced by professional administrators who were ex-coaches, players, and referees. The money got bigger, three man crews were the in thing, and patronage now became the order of the day. More guys wanted in and the commissioners ordered them to come to camps and clinics. A ladder was being formed and hundreds upon hundreds began to climb.

For Fred Hikel in 1978, just being alive was an accomplishment. Now he had to climb a ladder. He worked in the big tent again, and did just fine. But the commissioners said he had slipped, he had lost a step. There was too much money being made for them to care. Freddie never had or needed a sponsor. Now, at what would have been his prime, he was a high wire act without a net.

Fred Hikel officiated dozens of my games in high school and college. We became close friends through a commonality I was proud to possess. But even now as the fires are banked, my coaching instincts get to me and I resent his court demeanor and unwavering search for fairness. Damn it, he never once cut me a break. With Fred it was a matter of principle.

DR. HENRY SUTHERLAND
A Gentleman and A Scholar

"He was a giver, in a world of takers."

Wheeling College was just sixteen years old in 1971 when I became the athletic director and basketball coach, but the school was already faltering. Enrollment had dipped to under six hundred and the Admissions Department was under extreme pressure. The fifty-two acre campus was undeveloped. The faculty was underpaid and growing unruly. There was talk of the school closing down before it could even develop its mission.

The basketball team had three straight six win seasons and the players drove to away games in their own cars. The faculty wanted to drop basketball.

Despite their apprehension and disapproval, we spent money and moved forward. In my second year, Charles C. Currie, S.J. became President and, under his leadership, the College began to emerge from the black hole in which it seemed to be sinking. Neither of us were popular as the battle lines for survival were drawn. Currie began to raise money and poured cash into the Admissions effort.

In eight years we played winning basketball and spread the name of Wheeling College. The Cardinals went up against the likes of Georgetown, Pitt, South Carolina, Duquesne, St. Peter's, and Xavier, playing games in

Washington, DC, Baltimore, Philadelphia, Pittsburgh, Cincinnati, and Columbus. Keying off of our visibility, the Admissions Department began to bring in students.

With every step forward, the faculty would collectively posture itself, and lobby for the return of the high standards of Jesuit education. In actuality, the College was taking in all the warm bodies it could find. In retrospect our recruiting of basketball players in the 70's came nowhere near the open door policy that was occurring at the Catholic Harvard on the Potomac – Georgetown. Having come to Wheeling from Georgetown, Currie and I shared the same goal. He was on my side, win or tie.

My young wife was home with three pre-schoolers, having left a nice home and strong family ties in Baltimore. Money was tight and I was engrossed in my job. I did all the recruiting and all the coaching. The bloom came off the rose quickly.

During my second year a miracle appeared in the person of Henry Sutherland. An erudite scholar, he was the Chairman of the Modern Language Department. Henry spoke five languages fluently, taught class passionately, chain smoked, and knew absolutely nothing about basketball. Having disassociated himself from the political core of the faculty, he still remained arguably the most respected member of the Wheeling College community. As a young man he marched for Civil Rights in Mississippi and Alabama. He was sympathetic to our plight, especially to the black players appearing on this lily white campus.

Doc Sutherland became the Faculty Moderator of Athletics and a buffer between the faculty, administration and athletics. Over the next seven seasons he never missed a game. Henry tutored the players in all subjects and gave them a sense of responsibility and belonging. He made time for the players despite his own responsibilities as a Department Chairman and teacher. Henry looked the part of the disheveled professor. His office was cluttered with books, papers, musty ash trays, and fast food boxes. He wore some of the most outlandish wardrobe matchups you ever saw. It was all part of just being Henry. He always had time, compassion, and the right answer, for a student's problems.

After an early marriage, Doc had become a confirmed bachelor for life and now he was a basketball fan. On the nights we were off, Henry thought nothing of driving over 100 miles to see a West Virginia Conference game. While I scouted a game at nearby West Liberty, Henry might be down at Fairmont or Buckhannon. The next morning over much coffee and cigarettes, I would quiz Doc on what he saw the night before. Combining the word pictures he made – who the refs were, the actions and words of the coaches, the fan reaction, and how animated or agitated the specific play-ers were – along with a few pointed questions about where certain players were positioned, and the box score from the morning paper, I got a pretty damn good scouting report. All from a man who was just an observer. Doc had the human

Dr. Henry Sutherland went from knowing very little about basketball to the Wheeling College Cardinals biggest fan, never missing a game for seven consecutive seasons. He devoted nearly all of his later years to the school and team and will always be loved by those who knew him. Photo: Courtesy of Wheeling Jesuit University.

equation down pat.

Doc seemingly had favorites, but he really didn't. Whomever needed the most help got the most attention. At a time when chaos reigned and basketball was questioned, Henry's posture gave the players dignity and a sense of belonging. None of our players were ever short changed by Doc. He was so well respected that none of the players would ever take advantage of him. Still, Henry went into his own pocket on many occasion to make sure a player had money for a bus ticket home, food, supplies, and other basics.

In the Summer, Henry taught classes and drove to Pittsburgh to watch his beloved Pirates, but not before he put our on campus players through their daily drill. If he felt any of the players were being discriminated against, he would erupt in righteous indignation. He was intent on seeing to it that these players got an education and, for their efforts on behalf of the school, the benefit of the doubt. Because of his reputation on campus our faculty thought twice about the players. Grades in college many times boil down to "the benefit of the doubt." Henry saw to it that the rule was followed.

Doc Sutherland passed away in 1994 after a brief illness. He was special to all who came under his tutelage. He was a giver, not a taker – a rare commodity. I was never hesitant in recruiting athletes to come to Wheeling, despite what little we had to offer compared to other schools. I recruited them because I knew I could give them more – they would get to know Henry.

JO JO RETTON
The Coal Miner's Son

"Jo Jo could never look the other way. Instead, he just walked away."

Jo Jo Retton was the son of an Italian coal miner. He was born, raised, and educated in Fairmont, West Virginia. And, as he was wont to say, one day he would die in West Virginia.

In the meantime he became quite a basketball coach. In fact, he was a great one. In an 18 year period from 1963 to 1982 he managed to win 83% of his games at Fairmont State College in his home town. His team played in the West Virginia Conference as an NAIA member. The calibre of play was equal to lower levels of major college ball in the NCAA. His teams were the scourge of the Conference.

Jo Jo's coaching style can best be compared to football coach Vince Lombardi, though Paul Attner, then of the *Washington Post*, once compared him to Bobby Knight. Retton was a strict disciplinarian who ruled his players with an iron hand, twenty-four hours a day.

At one point in the mid-70's, Fairmont put together a home winning streak of over 80 games. Home was the Marion County Armory just outside of town. The College had no gym of which to speak. The Armory seated 3,500 and

117

everyone was shoehorned in place at least an hour before game time, stewing and fermenting. There was no parking lot. Pickup trucks, 4 x 4's, and RV's were strewn all over the countryside. For some of the really big games, the Fire Marshall would look the other way, and well over 4,000 would spill over into the aisles, concession areas, and hallways. During that decade there was no telling how much dirt and dust was tracked through those Armory doors. It surely contributed to the hazy film in the air. The balcony was ringed with screaming country folk and the smell of popcorn permeated the air. In the good seats around the court was Jo Jo's entourage, the Italian Colony of Fairmont. Jo Jo was God in this town.

At the other end of the court was a huge open stage. The basket seemed suspended in air. The depth perception was difficult to gauge. The rims were bent, the nets were dirty and the glass backboards always needed some of that Dick Vitale windex. On the stage, young kids with their popcorn and Cokes were having a ball taunting the visitors. It reminded me of the old Monastery(St. Joseph's) Hall. At the balcony end fans would lean over the rail to hiss and boo. In the early years the scoreboard had the old minute and second hands instead of the electric clock.

The visitor's locker room was tiny and dingy, reminiscent of a prison cell. You felt like the Christians in the bowels of the Roman Coliseum waiting for the Lions. Only it was the Fairmont Falcons. During the streak probably 90% of the referees were from the State of West Virginia. Most teams were intimidated before the opening tip. Then the execution would begin.

Jo Jo, year after year fielded a squad that moved the basketball with precision and grace. Seldom did the ball touch the floor and dribbling was kept to a minimum. Jo Jo invented the passing game before it was officially named. The

Flying Falcons, in their spotless white uniforms and shoes, formed a startling contrast to the dusty surroundings. There were always a few stud recruits sitting on the team bench. The program took on an intimidating aura of invincibility. Their fans cheered passionately and booed vehemently. Even the staunchest of these tiny West Virginia colleges would always come up short. The weak ones were swallowed up within minutes.

Jo Jo's coaching style consisted of a constant, plaintive banter with officials, always reminding them of who he was and where they were. Whenever a player would violate one of Jo Jo's Cardinal Rules, he was immediately yanked, publicly blistered, then sent to the end of the bench. No one was spared, the non-scoring sixth man to the Conference Player of the Year. The players knew better than to sulk, they nodded or listened stoically. Then they would be recycled back into the game. So, as the game progressed, Jo Jo was always teaching. They were always firmly under his thumb. For over a decade this show played to packed houses around the State with the same results. When Fairmont State lost it was big news.

Retton acquired players in many ways. Being a state school, there were no full athletic scholarships. West Virginia natives could qualify for different types of aide and poor kids always received grants. Jo Jo's Italian Colony provided booster club funds to recruit and supply the extras needed. Retton would take average players and develop them to the far limits of their potential. His value judgement was always based on his ability to control and dominate. If he could do that, he felt he could make the kid into a player. Jo Jo liked poor kids. Kids who had to depend on the program for survival. Most of his players would stay in town during the summer, go to school, work for the Italians and practice Jo Jo's precepts.

Added to this mix would be one or two supers who could play big time but had an impediment – bad grades, bad attitude, or poor home situations. As long as they could live with Jo Jo, they were welcome. Jo Jo never blatantly cheated, he just bent the rules a little. He never bought players. But as long as the players were controllable and productive, the Italians kept them in line with pizza, haircuts, movie money, basic clothing, and bus tickets home during the holidays. Senator Joe Manchin, a legendary figure in the West Virginia State Legislature, was known to frequent the Falcon locker room after big wins with his famous "Greenback Handshakes."

My personal experiences in eight years of competing with Jo Jo ran a true gamut of emotions. As a basketball purist, I considered him just a fair strategist and a so-so defensive coach. If you slowed down the tempo he would not press you. There was no shot clock in those days. Thus, he allowed poor opponents to stay close. He just bitched about the slowdowns but never came after you. His defense was very cautious and basic. Jo Jo was conservative by nature. His teams seldom got into foul trouble, boxed out well, and defended the perimeter. But, on offense they were a machine with fluid ball movement, limited dribbling and impeccable shot selection. The best players always ended up shooting the most shots, which was no small order. Some players were only allowed to shoot open layups. They were in great condition and never beat themselves. When I had my best teams, we ran with them and lost. With less talent we would stay in the game until the end.

One night in the aforementioned Marion County Armory we took the Falcons into overtime. We were quick and could press. Most teams refused to press Fairmont, fearing their speed and precision, so they retreated to the perimeter and took their chances. On this night we decided to press them,

Jo Jo Retton was one of the most successful coaches in the history of the West Virginia Basketball Conference, yet he was content to remain a Big Fish in a Small Pond. Photos: Courtesy of the Fairmont State Athletic Department.

121

balls to the wall. The results were shocking. The Falcons, being used to passive defenses, were not used to a team playing up in the passing lanes. They threw to the open spots that were vacated by players moving away because of our overplay. The first half ended with 15 Falcon turnovers. They usually completed an entire game with less than ten miscues. At the halftime buzzer, which was a full second late, Fairmont's Davey Moore threw in a 50-footer to give them the lead. There upon, a full decade before the General, I unleashed one of the Armory's finest metal chairs into orbit. It hit at the foul line and bounced around on its legs like a bucking bronco. The fans unleashed their boos and the kids in the balcony gave us a popcorn shower on the way to the catacombs.

After losing in OT, the Armory manager appeared at our locker room door with a bill for the twisted chair. In no uncertain terms I told him to give the chair to Jo Jo as repayment for the blackboard he put his fist through at our place the year before.

But there was a big chink in Retton's armor. He was definitely a control freak. He would never fly in a plane and the many years Fairmont went to the Nationals in Kansas City, the team flew out ahead as he drove out in one of the Italians' Cadillacs. Despite their great regular season records, other than in 1968 when they reached the National Finals, Jo Jo's record in post season play was dismal. They pounded the hell out of the West Virginia Conference schools, but they rarely traveled and never played major teams. Retton never talked about "winning it all" and, somehow, this reluctance was transferred to the psyche of the players. Whenever they traveled outside the boundaries of West Virginia they were vulnerable.

Back in the 70's when Duquesne was a strong program, we played them to a standstill in the Pittsburgh Civic Center, losing at the buzzer. Not long thereafter we lost a nine point game to Fairmont, prompting Falcon assistant Mike Arcure to infer that Fairmont might be better than Duquesne. I replied to Mike, "The only way to find out is to play them." Of course Fairmont would never consider playing a bigger school and it hurt them on the national level. Retton was content to stay a big fish in a small pond and he was quite successful at it.

In the semi-finals of the 1978 West Virginia Conference Tournament in Charleston, Wheeling College and Paul Baker beat Jo Jo's Falcons 69-60 in front of 7,000 fans, including the Governor and most of the Italian population of Fairmont. The next year we also beat them at the buzzer in Wheeling. They were memorable games for me.

In 1979 Fairmont State built an on-campus, all purpose fieldhouse seating 5,000. Jo Jo was given a state of the art locker room facility and no major college program had better digs. The Italians put in a big refrigerator stocked with pro- volone, pepperoni, and cold beer. Even though he bragged about it and showed it off to his lesser peers, this place was not of Jo Jo's making. It turned out to be an overkill culture shock. Jo Jo flourished in the Marion County Armory, trans- porting the dirty basketballs and sleepy players in beat up station wagons for early morning workouts. Austerity was Jo Jo's glue – it was his middle name, his West Virginia, Italian pick and shovel upbringing. The change was unnat- ural and it upset the balance. The Armory had made it all come together.

At this time Retton was considered for the West Virginia job and many of the politicians in the State seemed to be behind his candidacy. He lost out to Gale Catlett. Failing to get the only job he seemed destined for, he found himself frustrated and living in a changing world. It was a little too much for him. He clashed with the new president and, two years into the new building, Jo Jo Retton resigned. He remained at Fairmont as a tenured Physical Education instructor and his career was later remembered in a full-length *Sports Illustrated* feature article.

Catlett has done well at West Virginia so there is no second guess there. The players of the 80's and 90's are more difficult and spoiled. Television hoops, the deterioration of our cities, and the early influence of AAU off-season play has rendered the modern player practically uncoachable. Coaches must now be political. The biggest asset for the modern coach is to know when to look the other way. Jo Jo could never look the other way. Instead, he just walked away.

Joe Retton was a gym teacher by trade. His fundamental training in basketball was so basic it could have come from Phys-Ed teaching manuals. But when you added in all his attention to detail, discipline, and that intimidating persona, you had the formula for great success.

Throughout the length and breadth of this country, over decades and millions of games, there have been many coaches who were truly remarkable, yet relatively unknown outside of their own area. Joe Retton was one of those coaches. And, there is a handful of great Italian coaches; Calipari, Carnessecca, Massimino, Pitino, and Valvano. Household names, they could have all learned a thing or two from the Coal Miner's Son. I did.

GRANT HILL
The Baltimore Connection

"Baltimore basketball guru Paul Baker told me even before Grant Hill graduated from South Lakes High School in Reston, Va., that the youngster, who had just announced he would attend Duke, would become the greatest player in Blue Devils history." -- Bill Tanton's "Inside Stuff", Baltimore Evening Sun, April 9, 1992.

I first saw Grant Hill at the Five Star Basketball Camp in the mountains around Honesdale, Pennsylvania. It was Labor Day weekend in 1988. He was a rising junior. August-Honesdale is the last stop on the summer camp junket. Howard Garfinkel's Summer Sayonara. Traditionally it is New York City Week as all of Gotham's best gravitate for one last blast of exposure.

The week ends with the All Star Game, played outdoors in the cold mountain air. In a fleeting hour Summer will come to a rude closure. The sky is pitch dark framing an orange peel moon as the entire camp populace, some 400 strong, ring the court, shivering. Coaches, scouts, evaluators, and assorted hoop junkies lurk in the shadows for a last look. The players loosen up and their warm breath meets the evening chill forming halos of steam. It is too cold for bas-

125

ketball.

Grant Hill stands alone, kind of pale, still lanky and fuzzy cheeked. Even his clean shoes have that suburban look. There is no hint of greatness. In fact he reminds so many of those white suburban impostors. Lots of hype and no game. Maybe now we have a black one on our hands.

In the makeshift bleachers sits his mother, waiting to transport him back to the real world. She also looks out of place, like parents do when they come, caring about their kids.

The other participants are some of New York's "finest," walking the walk and talking the talk. Scarred up raga-muffins whose ravaged playground brogans tell their own story.

The All Star game begins as a selfish free for all. Three minutes go by and Hill has not touched the ball. He moves up and down the court, gauging. A jump shot is launched from the top of the key, straight but hard off the back rim. Grant appears as if on wings, meeting the ball at its highest point with one hand. High above the nine figures below, he squares in mid-air and gently drops the ball down into the basket. A ten-foot finger roll. There was a hush, a murmur, then wild applause. I rubbed my eyes but the vision was gone. Elgin Baylor, Connie Hawkins, and Julius Erving came across my screen. The rest of the game played out in a trance as everyone there kept rewinding back to that moment. Grant Hill had officially "come out." From that moment on, I began to view him in a different light. The more I learned about him, the more impressed I became and soon I predict-ed greatness, as recounted by this April 9, 1992 excerpt from Bill Tanton's "The Inside Stuff" column in the *Baltimore Evening Sun*.

Baltimore basketball guru **Paul Baker** told me
even before **Grant Hill** graduated from South Lakes

High School in Reston, Va., that the youngster, who had just announced he would attend Duke, would become the greatest player in Blue Devils history.

Having seen **Danny Ferry, Mark Alarie, Johnny Dawkins, Dick Groat** and **Art Heyman,** I knew that was quite a prediction. But after watching Hill in action as Duke repeated its NCAA championship, I'm starting to believe Baker. That's a pretty good prediction – even for a guru.

Great players have spent thousands of hours from the time they could walk, developing their "craft and persona" on the court. We have heard the stories about Bird and West at the barn door basket, Oscar on the Indianapolis dirt flats, and all the products of the "City Game." Others played in great high school programs under legendary coaches. Grant did none of the above. We are in the "Electronic Generation." Kids don't do anything anymore for countless hours, unless it's sleeping or video related activity. They see sports on TV then they go out and try to do it themselves. Grant Hill got his first taste of hoops on the tube. He said, "I can do that,"

The Baltimore Connection: Harvey Kasoff (center), the son of Morris Kasoff, flanked by Calvin and Grant Hill, when Grant was just a Freshman in College.
Photo: Harvey Kasoff's private collection.

and "that too," and also "that" and "that." Then he went out and did it. If you can come up with a better explanation I want to hear it. This kid was a natural. He was born to play.

Of course the genealogy factor is clearly on his side. Calvin Hill was a truly outstanding star with the NFL's Cowboys, Redskins, and Browns, playing in four Pro Bowls and two Super Bowls. Lean, strong, fast and tough with great hands, Calvin was also durable, level headed, and humble. No doubt young Grant was fixated on his daddy early. Janet McDonald Hill is an intelligent, highly educated woman with strong family roots and a global view on life. She has created her own business dynasty and legacy. How did fate bring this 20th Century fairy tale about?

I have known Harvey Kasoff for close to fifty years. We met in high school, played some amateur hoops and crossed paths from time to time. We reconnected in the 80's. Harvey's father, Morris Kasoff owned Key Wine and Liquor Distributors on old DeSoto Road in Southwest Baltimore and, at one time, he owned a piece of the Baltimore Bullets. At the age of twelve, Harvey became the Bullet ball boy. There he met the sports idol of his life, Buddy Jeannette, who was eventually inducted into the Basketball Hall of Fame in 1994 – no small thanks to Harvey's constant lobbying. Harvey had two sons, Eddie and Mitchell, who played collegiately at Johns Hopkins and Maryland after record setting high school careers at Pikesville High School.

Morris Kasoff started Jim Parker and Art Donovan off in the liquor business where they would eventually earn more money than they ever did on the football field. Through the efforts of Dr. William Wade, Morris Kasoff and Jim Parker were made aware of a young kid in need of help. Calvin Hill,

128

then fifteen was ready to enter Sollers Point Jr. High School, an all black school in the Dundalk area of Baltimore County. The Hill family lived in a black section called Turner Station which had sprung up between the World Wars to house Bethlehem Steel employees. Henry Hill and his wife Vivian raised Calvin in a structured religious atmosphere. In addition to being an outstanding athlete, he was an even better student. He was already thinking Divinity School. Through the Schenley Foundation, Morris Kasoff recommended Calvin for a scholarship. He qualified with flying colors and matriculated to the exclusive Riverdale Prep School in Riverdale, New York. The rest is history. At Yale he graduated with honors and was an All American selection. Had he stayed in Baltimore, he might have been discovered by Mt. St. Joe, Calvert Hall, or Gilman – then off to Notre Dame or Penn State. He may still have had a great professional football career, but he probably would have never met Janet McDonald, who was a student at Wellesley near Yale and, we would not have had Grant Hill as we know him today.

In 1994, as Hill was preparing to lead Duke into another Final Four and, ultimately, another National Championship, Tanton reminded me of my earlier prediction and, on March 29, quoted me in his column once again.

> Amazingly, when Grant Hill came out of South Lakes High School in Virginia and chose Duke over North Carolina, Baltimore basketball guru Paul Baker told me Hill would become "the greatest player ever to wear a Duke jersey."
>
> Yesterday, I reminded Baker, now a Washington Bullets scout, of his prediction.
>
> "I think it's going to happen," Baker said. "He's right there now with Laettner and Hurley. If Duke wins the whole thing – which means Grant Hill will have played great in these last two games – Grant will go down as the best."

Interestingly, Baker is preparing a scouting report for the Bullets on Hill.

"The kid is a winner," Baker says. "He elevates all the players around him. He's 6-8, weights 225 and has long arms.

"He's the best college player in America today. I recommend the Bullets draft him No. 1 if we can get the chance. Hill could start for any team in the NBA and do any job they need done."

Now, here is my actual Scouting Report, given to the Bullets, on Grant Hill:

GRANT HILL - DUKE - 6'8/225 (LEGIT SIZE) SR.
Point Guard/Shooting Guard/Small Forward
Observed vs. Maryland–March 2, 1994 @ College Park
LOTTERY PICK – Between 1 and 5
OVERALL
Hill has done everything asked of him at Duke. As the team chemistry changed, so did Grant in order to make the team better. At one time or another has played all ten positions on the floor. $\left(\begin{smallmatrix} 5 \text{ on Offense} \\ 5 \text{ on Defense} \end{smallmatrix}\right)$ Combines the gifts of athleticism and basketball skill as effectively as any college player I have ever seen. He is as cerebral as Gola, Bradley, or Bird and just as versatile as Magic Johnson and Oscar.

He is so modest, proper and unassuming, and has played for the perfect coach in the perfect program, that his contributions are muted. And despite some prodigious dunks, his game does not outwardly compare favorably with current standards of evaluation.

But be forewarned, there are no smoke and mirrors with this guy. He is a pure basketball machine with the greatest attitude known to man tacked on for good measure.
OFFENSE
This year he is single handedly moving Duke toward a third National title in four years, playing point

130

guard. At this writing, Duke is a blazing 22-3, averaging close to 80 points and shooting nearly 40% on the 3's, because they are so selective on offense. Hill is orchestrating this style, possession by possession. At 6'8"/225 with a wide body and long arms, no one can effectively press him. His size allows him to "look over the top of the defense," view the action and make the right decisions. He runs the team like Magic Johnson. Under Coach K's mandate, Hill dishes the ball out to the right player at the right time. There is very little pressure on the other Duke players. It is all on his shoulders and he handles it well.

He is a slashing driver with a quick first step and a variety of spin moves not seen in too many 6'8" players. He penetrates and finishes. Maryland's Johnny Rhodes, a 6'-4$_{1/2}$" inner city kid with super quick hands was backpedaling all night attempting to guard Hill. Grant Hill has the knack of hitting the open man just as he comes free.

A 70% foul shooter, he is currently shooting 38% on treys, while averaging 17.0 PPG - 6.3 RBS. - 6.0 ASSISTS.

In the NBA – he can start the break off the boards, lead the break off the dribble, or finish the break with a monster slam from day one.

I would place little emphasis on the evaluation of his shooting. His detractors will point to the fact that he is not a knockdown shooter. Yet he is more than adequate. Like Magic Johnson, he does so many great things that shooting becomes secondary. He leaves that to the mere mortals.

DEFENSE

Would have trouble guarding a 6'3" and under whippet. But he can cover 2's, 3's, and some power forwards. Knows the team defense concept to a T. Hellacious rebounder and shot blocker. Because of foul trouble worries, he holds back on blocking shots. But he has the wingspan, timing, and leaping ability to be an intimidator – even on the NBA level. Currently at 125 career blocks and over 200 steals.

He also gets loose balls and makes steals in the open court. I would classify Hill as a defensive stopper.

CONCLUSION

Grant Hill is a winner and he elevates the players around him. His great physical skills are minimized by the program he plays in, and by his own vanilla style. HE IS THE BEST COLLEGE BASKETBALL PLAYER IN AMERICA TODAY. Seldom has a player come along who possesses size, skill, exceptional mental ability, and emotional ability. I WOULD DRAFT HIM NUMBER ONE WITHOUT A SECOND THOUGHT. He can start as a rookie for any NBA team at whatever position they need filled. The more structured the team concept, the better he would be.

Grant Hill was born in Dallas and raised in Reston, Virginia, but his roots run deep in Baltimore through his paternal grandparents and his father. He may not be the second coming of Michael Jordan (that mold was broken after MJ), but he is a legitimate NBA Superstar who is still rising. And, it all goes back to the day when a guy named Morris Kasoff answered a phone call and helped a kid from Baltimore.

ISAIAH "BUNNY" WILSON
Scoring Machine

"Bunny Wilson attracted more people to Rogers Avenue than a bad day at Pimlico," -- the late Charley Eckman.

Isaiah "Bunny" Wilson was the 6th man on his high school team – no more, no less. His coach at Southern High School in Philadelphia was Bill Esher, who ran the highly successful Wildwood Basketball Clinic in the summers. We became friends and he began to send me players at Baltimore University, where I was the head coach in the middle 60's.

After Wilson graduated from Southern, he spent a year at Temple Prep to improve his grades and then Esher recommended him to me. Bunny's grades were still suspect and he seemed to be an unpolished player in a city loaded with prospects, but Bill's word was good enough for me.

I took Mr. Wilson sight unseen. He appeared one summer day at Baltimore's Penn Station with all his earthly belongings in a straw suitcase. With me that day was my two year old son Steve, he and Bunny became fast friends, a relationship that still continues today. As Baltimore University had no dorms, I found him a place to live off of Old York Road in the Blessed Sacrament parish. His landlady was Mrs. Augusta Thistle, who gave him his own room in her rowhouse. Bunny spent two years with her. She was Gene Shue's mother-in-law. In those days I was part real estate agent, securing lodging for all of the out of town players.

Bunny was better than advertised. At that time freshmen were not eligible for varsity play, so he proceeded to average close to 40-points per game for the frosh. Most notable was his 50-point explosion versus the Navy Plebes and a 35-point game against DeMatha in a prelim to the Bullet-Laker game at the Civic Center. Jerry West and Butch van Breda Kolf, the Laker's coach, sat in the first row and watched intently. Butch would later coach Bunny in the NBA.

Wilson was a skinny, long armed swing man at 6'2", 160 pounds out of high school. His game was school yard in nature. He was a one-on-one half court player who would kill you from inside 15-feet. Possessing the pump fakes, spins, and hesitation moves of Earl Monroe, he had a feathery touch inside and out. Despite the great freshman display, he was far from being a complete player. His school yard habits kept him from putting the ball on the floor for more than two dribbles. He was more comfortable backing his defender in, then using his bag of tricks. He continued this style as a sophomore, averaging 23 points per game as B.U. notched its first winning season in a decade. That Summer things changed for Bunny. His home was the basketball court. We developed a ball handling and dribbling regimen for him. He went at it full tilt, up and down the court – spinning, hesitating, going behind his back and through his legs, dribbling high and low, always with his head up so he could see the entire court.

He went to Bob Cousy's Camp as a counselor. There he played with some of the Celtic rookies and impressed Cousy with his potential. When he came back for his junior year, Bunny was a bonafide guard. He no longer had to originate

Isaiah "Bunny" Wilson was a scoring machine, who came to B.U. from Philadephia. In three varsity seasons with the Bees, he averaged just under 29 points per game.
Photo: Courtesy of the University of Baltimore Archives.

the play with his back to the basket, although that weapon was still there for him. Now he could put the ball on the floor with either hand, get into the lane, stop on a dime, and deliver that feathery jump shot over an outmaneuvered opponent. He also became a great passer off the penetration, making him hard to double team.

As a junior he averaged 34-points per game, making second team All American. He led Baltimore University to its best season since the 1930's with an 18-7 record. We beat major colleges George Washington and Canisius plus arch rival Loyola.

His senior year was marred by a severe ankle sprain that kept him out of eight games. However, the NBA scouts knew about him and every time a visiting team was at the Civic Center, invariably we would have visitors observing our practices. Bunny Wilson was a big time scoring machine. In three years of varsity play he averaged just under 29-points per game.

Today, over 25 years later, he remains in the Top Ten of Division II all-time scorers. He was a sight to behold, scoring every way possible. He shot over 75% from the foul line. He scored off steals, loose balls, and got garbage baskets off the glass. One-on-one, he could get in the lane like a hot knife through butter. Off the dribble he had that stop on a dime pull up jumper, and lastly if you played him loose he could hit the equivalent of the modern trey with ease. He dumped some big numbers on shocked opponents. The night Earl Lloyd, the Pistons' head scout, showed up, Bunny dropped 51 on Roanoke, a Top Ten team. The Pistons eventually drafted Bunny in the 2nd round of the 1971 NBA Draft, the 28th overall pick. This was not bad for kid who had no place to go after high school.

There was always the question of how such a talent could end up at such a ragamuffin school. We played our games at the old St. Paul's School on Rogers Avenue near Pimlico. The white stucco barn held around 400-500 and the court was 84' x 42'. The walls were on top of the players, but Bunny and the Bees drew. Charley Eckman, who refereed some of our games, stated, "Bunny Wilson attracted more people to Rogers Avenue than a bad day at Pimlico."

During the early 60's Baltimore University was not integrated. Most of the athletes were from low to middle income families. Everyone was seeking their own identity. Having grown up in an Italian neighborhood in South Philly, Bunny knew how to mix in with the rednecks and ethnic folks. His warm personality and unique athletic ability translated into easy acceptance.

In retrospect, Wilson's rise at B.U. was so sudden and so unexpected, it was hard to grasp how great he was at the time. He may be the best player to have ever played local college basketball in Baltimore. In fact, Snuffy Smith says, "In the last twenty-five years, few if any local colleges have had a player with his offensive skills and abilities. He could take his man to 15-feet, pull up, and shoot over him, at will."

From here, Wilson played professionally in the NBA and ABA for a total of two years, much longer than anyone could have expected considering his humble beginnings.

VINCE BAGLI

Born To Be A Broadcaster – In Baltimore

". . . he never misses a beat, taking you back to pleasant days gone by, placing you somewhere in your old living room or in a favorite lawn chair."

Vince Bagli was born in Hamilton a long time ago. He never left Baltimore, a town with working class roots. The son of a doctor who was a sports enthusiast, it was only natural that he would follow. As a kid Vince played the game, then replayed it in the streets and alleys of his neighborhood as an announcer. By the time he finished Loyola High School and matriculated to Loyola College, he knew his vocation would encompass sports. In 1949 the Loyola Greyhounds of Lefty Reitz, starring Jim Lacy, were in Kansas City for the NAIA Nationals. The game was not broadcast, but was available off the AP wire ticker tape. Bagli recreated the game and gave his play-by-play to the spellbound student body who had assembled en masse in Evergreen Gym.

A career was born.

Along with John Steadman, Vince Bagli has chronicled the Baltimore sports scene as its unofficial archivist, purist and advocate par excellence. In the presence of these two, anything and everything about our sports heritage, for well

139

over a half century, can be recalled and put into perspective. Often times during his illustrious career Bagli had opportunities to leave Baltimore for the brighter lights. Two of his close friends, Frank Cashen and Jim McKay, did with great success. But raising a large family and enjoying his job here were enough for Vince.

With his sense of the City, both past and present, Vince easily became the spokesman for the working class stiff, as well as the Roland Park blueblood. He is the only guy I know who could play golf one morning at Clifton Park, then tee off as a guest of a Caves Valley Member later in the week. He could get a standing "O" at Steelworkers' Hall or the Bachelor's Cotillion. This universal acclaim can be traced to his humility and graciousness. He never strayed far from his roots. He always gave the common man and the superstar equal time. Often at a public function, your conversation with Vince would be interrupted by a "celebrity or big timer," but never would he allow this intrusion without introducing both parties and keeping the common man in the loop. "There it is," Bagli's success and charm over the decades was his ability to keep the common man in the loop.

In his closing years on Channel 11, I would sometimes hear lukewarm comments from sports fans I knew. Invariably, to a man, they were not Baltimore natives. They wanted to hear glib commentary with hi-tech glitz, but Vince Bagli is pure Baltimore – class without class consciousness. I have been privileged to know Vince for just about 50 years, but our connection goes back even further. In 1935 at old St. Joseph's Hospital in downtown Baltimore, I was delivered by Dr. Francis Bagli, Vince's father. Small world this Baltimore. In 1949 I answered a sports question Vince asked on radio station WBMD. It was a question only he would ask, and only I could answer. I won two movie tickets and a long friendship began. In the early 50's he did high school football from the stadium on radio, giving me a bigger plug than I deserved. To this day he still remembers my high school number. That's Vince. He raised a toast at my wedding and continued to "boost my career" through his media positions with the *News American* and Channel 11, never letting the Colts and Orioles smother out the little guy.

Retired and out of the public eye, Vince can now relax and rest easy. During days past, he paid a price for his time and energy, doing so many events and benefits for the community. He still makes cameo appearances as a guest speaker or master of ceremonies. On these occasions he never misses a beat, taking you back to pleasant days gone by, placing you somewhere in your old living room or in a favorite lawn chair. His attention to detail and total recall are always

Vince Bagli, with his down home charm and sincerity, became a hero to Baltimore's working class sports fans, whom he always "kept in the loop." This same charm also endeared him to the "so-called" big timers such as former President George Bush, who Bagli calls, "one of my favorites."
Photo: Courtesy of Vince Bagli's private collection.

refreshing.

As he enjoys his retirement with his lovely wife Jean, Vince can be found on the local golf courses. He never felt inclined to become a country club guy. What would the steelworkers think? Keith Mills carries the torch on Channel 2 with his devotion to Baltimore and the common man. But, there will never be another Vince Bagli. Hit 'em straight Vince.

PAUL DIAKOULAS
Zorba

"As they approached, Zorba adroitly grabbed the fish from "Woody" and in a flash whipped out a sharp knife from his boot (no sandals were allowed on road trips), split the fish, deboned it, poured on oil and vinegar from the salad cruets, and, in less time than you could say Jesus Christ Superstar, began to eat the raw fish."

Paul Diakoulas (dee-a-cool-us) graduated from Poly around 1967. He was long and lean, muscular and athletic, but possessed no fundamental basketball skills. Poly had a good team so he was history early. But he continued to play basketball on the sandlots and became proficient. He enrolled at Baltimore University. We too had a good team, but Paul was lucky, our numbers were thin. Some days we had trouble rustling up ten healthy players and he provided an extra body.

When he first enveloped the threshold of my tiny office door, I was not prepared for the shock. Granted it was the 60's and America was in turmoil. You expected nonconformity. My players had longish hair and far out habits, but we met at a common ground based on mutual respect and a strong will to win. I was flexible. Paul's look, however, was

143

different and stunning. He had shoulder length hair and a unkempt beard. Wearing a raggy undershirt, cut off jeans and thong sandals with no socks, he gave off a distinctive odor, which was later traced to his many hours working at his family's fish stall in Lexington Market. Instead of being a hippie, this guy was more like a caveman or mountain man. His voice had a deep foreign inflection. I was in the company of a teenager who sounded like an old sea captain. Coming from a home where nothing but Greek was ever spoken gave him that inflection. He was an old world throwback and I liked him immediately as did his new teammates. He was quickly named Zorba, the only Greek name we knew. We began to domesticate him, trimming the hair and beard just a bit. Between school, work at the market, and women, he worked in our practice regimen.

Zorba was always the last man on the floor, as he would speed up the JFX in his red convertible from the Market. We would hear the gym door slam, seconds later the fish aroma wafted up onto our second floor court, quickly followed by Zorba himself. The players loved him and one of the reasons was that with Zorba on board, none of them could ever be considered the most "far out." Paul's parents were born on the island of Rhodes in a fishing village called Lindos. He was brought up Greek. The American came slowly. He was a hard worker and hustler. He could run like the wind and jump to the moon. At 6'-5" and 185-pounds, his wingspan and quickness made him seem larger. If only he could catch the ball and remember the plays. But as the year went on he began to improve and contribute to our fine season.

On a road trip down South to Roanoke College an unusual event occurred. Our team was having breakfast in the campus dining hall and a few of Roanoke's fraternity kids came over to rap. One guy was a mischievous "pledge master" who looked like Woody Allen. He playfully gave us a hard time and teased Zorba, calling him "Jesus Christ Superstar." Later that day we were sitting together in a quiet part of the dining hall eating our pregame meal. Coeds were forming a line for dinner and, all of a sudden, they began screaming and scattering in all directions. As we looked up, there was "Woody Allen" barefoot, clad only in a jock strap, enveloped in a leopard skin cape, brandishing a smelly, raw fish. In his other hand was a noisy rattle that he kept shaking. He was followed by a bunch of his frat brothers. They came toward us in our little corner, hoping to have some fun at our expense.

As they approached, Zorba adroitly grabbed the fish from "Woody" and in a flash whipped out a sharp knife from his boot (no sandals were allowed on road trips), filetéd the fish, deboned it, poured on oil and vinegar from the salad cruets, and, in less time than you could say Jesus Christ Superstar, began to eat the raw fish. The team burst into unbridled laughter as "Woody" and his boys exited in total consternation.

A clean-cut Zorba, at least by his standards (5th from right, just over my left shoulder), poses with his 1969-70 Baltimore Bee teammates above. In the inset, however, the modern day Zorba emerges from the Aegean Sea in his native Greek town of Lindos with the catch of the day. Zorba spends nearly every Summer day spear fishing several miles off the Aegean coast with nothing more than a wetsuit, a snorkle and his spear gun. Photos: Baltimore Bees Courtesy of the University of Baltimore Archives, Zorba photo from Paul Baker's private collection.

145

Years later Paul went back to his ancestral home in Lindos, reopened his parents house and turned it into a very trendy disco by the sea. He continued to grow as a player, spending a decade as a viable star in the Major League of Greece for the Olympiakos Club. They played all over Europe. Paul has lived in Greece for the past 25 years. He has never permanently returned to America. His only visits are when he reverses roles with his parents and visits them. Since his retirement he now lives in Switzerland during the Winter and coaches professional basketball. In the summers he returns to his beloved Lindos with his wife Christa and teenage daughter Selina.

Almost every day he swims several miles out into the Aegean, with no tank, and deep sea fishes with a spear gun. The reason Paul refuses to use an air tank, "It wouldn't be fair to the fish," he says. I would not have believed it except that in the Summer of 1994 we visited Paul and his family.

Always his own man, he was never an American. And despite living his formative years in the States, he was drawn back to his Greece, the sea, and the hardwood.

WALTER YOUSE & SHERIFF FOWBLE
Baltimore Baseball Legends

". . .the major reason for Baltimore's success in amateur baseball is, unquestionably, the leadership of Sheriff Fowble and Walter Youse for the last fifty years."

For more than a half century two men were personally responsible for the great development of baseball talent in the Baltimore area. For decades they recruited the cream of the crop, then taught and nurtured them into reaching their full potential, on and off the field. Other programs played up to meet the challenge thus making Baltimore a great baseball area. Every big league team had a card carrying scout who lived in Baltimore. In the decades of the 40's, 50's, and 60's, when minor league baseball was still in full bloom, hundreds of Baltimore sandlotters "went away" to try their skills in the professional arena.

Walter Youse and Sterling "Sheriff" Fowble were two different people, but with one common interest – baseball.

Sheriff, who wore that big John Wayne cowboy hat, certainly looked like a sheriff. Actually, his dad was the Sheriff of Carroll County. He concentrated on the younger prospects in the 14-16 age range, winning big year after year. Fowble's teams were always well dressed, well coached, and classy.

Over the years they played under the sponsorship of High's Ice Cream, High A.C., Gordon's Stores, G&M Scrap, Highland Lanes, Hi-Landers, and Highland Federal, which still sponsors the team today, coached by one of Fowble's former players, Bill Becker.

Here are the highlights of Fowble's legendary coaching record:

- 46 Consecutive Winning Seasons
- 1,660 Wins - 339 Losses (a .830 Winning Percentage)
- 77 League Championships
- 24 Baltimore City Championships
- 3 State Championships
- 4 Regional Championships
- 3 National Championships

Fowble and his lovely wife/scorekeeper/confidant Virginia, provided a comfortable, home away from home, atmosphere. Sheriff taught fundamentals and knew the game. He was a scout for the Cincinnati Reds and later the New York Mets. As a kid, I always played a little harder against Fowble's teams because they were the best. And therein lies Sheriff's biggest gift, his efforts in the game lifted up everyone, even the opponents. I got to know him better years later when I coached basketball. Sheriff officiated some of my games and I came to realize what a caring person he was and how lucky his players were to have played for him.

Today his former players, along with Virginia, have formed a foundation in honor of Sheriff, who passed away in 1991. The Fowble Foundation raises educational funds and awards them to deserving youngsters each year. And the team, under Becker's leadership, still makes its home field at Patterson #1, now named Fowble Field.

In the fifty years of his stewardship Sheriff touched the

lives of more than six hundred boys. About one hundred of his players signed professional contracts. This family operation of comraderie reminds me of Dean Smith and his North Carolina basketball program, but they have only existed for thirty-seven years.

Walter Youse is also quite a personality. A little more gruff and rough around the edges, I always envisioned what the great John McGraw must have been like when I thought of Walter. Youse is a strong disciplinarian and he goes back to the 30's when he managed in the Eastern Shore League. He still coaches Leone's and has scouted for the Milwaukee Brewers, and currently the Orioles. Highly respected, his every word is "leaned on." Today, at 84, Youse is still going strong and here are some highlights from his resume, which is too lengthy for this piece:

- Over 300 Players Signed to Pro Contracts
- 20 National Titles with Leone's

The late Sheriff Fowble (left) and Walter Youse flank former Oriole manager Joe Altobelli at the 1984 Tops In Sports Baseball Banquet held at the Towson Center.
Photos: Courtesy of Mrs. Virginia Fowble.

149

- 12 American Legion Titles
- Several MSA Titles
- Coached the following current major league pitchers: Jay Hamilton, Todd Jones, Paul Schuey, Wayne Gomes, and Denny Neagle.

Many of Walter's disciples, including Bernie Walter, Mel Montgomery, Snooky Binder, George Henderson, and Jimmy Foit (my old quarterback for "Saturday's Hero"), are still around town and teaching top notch baseball.

Currently, Youse coaches Kevin Olkowski, who played at Calvert Hall and is currently on a baseball scholarship at West Virginia. I brought Kevin's dad, Chuck Olkowski, down from Philadelphia in the 60's to play basketball at B.U. Chuck was a late bloomer. Cut from his high school team, he grew to 6'-8", had a great college career and almost stuck with the Bullets. Kevin is also a late bloomer who throws right and hits left. Walter, a shrewd, hard to please judge of talent, likes him. The kid just might make it to the bigs.

This town always had "good baseball." One of the factors was the plethora of great fields at Patterson, Clifton, Herring Run, Bloomingdale, Burdick, Slentz, Spring Grove, Carroll and Gambrills. Youse also notes the inspiration of the Orioles' presence in Baltimore, going back to the 30's. He says that in days gone by, sandlot baseball used to get great local coverage in the *News Post* and *Sunpapers*, thus inspiring kids. And, of course, Baltimore always had great instructional camps and clinics.

But if you ask me and thousands of other knowledgeable baseball people, the major reason for Baltimore's success in amateur baseball is, unquestionably, the leadership of Sheriff Fowble and Walter Youse for the last fifty years. With Sheriff's legacy currently continuing and Walter still coaching, Baltimore baseball is still going strong.

Section III

Coaching and Beyond. . .

TOWSON CATHOLIC OWLS
We Almost Captured Lightning in a Bottle

"This must have been how people in Indiana embraced the game."

In 1961 I was fortunate to be named a U.S. History teacher, athletic director, and head basketball coach at Towson Catholic High School. I was 26.

The only Catholic co-ed high school in the Baltimore area, there was a quiet strength and spirit to this parish school attached to the Immaculate Conception Grade School and Church. The high school served a sole purpose – to provide an opportunity to continue a Catholic education for parish kids and anyone else who couldn't qualify academically or financially for any of the more prestigious area schools.

Rev. Martin Schwalenberg was the assistant pastor to the fabled Monsignor Joseph Nelligan. Fr. Marty was a sports oriented guy who had connections throughout the City's Catholic parishes. Thus, a steady stream of players always found their way up to Ware Avenue.

In the 40's, Fr. Marty brought in Al Barthelme as his coach and, from that point on, TC was in the thick of the local hoops scene. Among Barthelme products was Gene Shue, TC's greatest player to date.

When I arrived the spirit at the school was high. The gym seated 400 and on many occasions, lots more were shoe-horned in around the court. Every student exercised their right to attend home games. Our cheerleaders painted huge signs that hung from the walls. The nuns would huddle in the North corner of the stands, praying the rosary. Kids in the first row would have their feet nearly touching the side-lines and the baselines were just three feet from the gym walls. The baskets hung out from the wall and the back-boards were fan shaped. The court was only 84-feet long, but the close quarters and packed houses shrunk the dimensions even more.

We used this home court to our advantage and pressed full-court the entire game. Teams with much more talent were scared to death of us. We were basically tiny and all white, but lots of newspaper coverage made us seem larger than life and we played up to our image. All of our games were emotional events. The cheerleaders, nuns and coeds screamed, cheered and cried, win or lose. During those years we held the edge over all the prominent Catholic schools – Loyola, St. Joe and Calvert Hall. In fact, we never lost to Loyola which was a great source of pride for all of our stu-dents. This must have been how people in Indiana embraced the game.

Our pressing defense led to exciting uptempo games as the Owls averaged over 75 points per game in my last two years as coach. During this time we were 52-10 (26-6 and 26-4) with no one over 6'-4".

I coached for another 15 years but never had another team quite like those TC Owls. We almost captured lightning in a bottle. Losing by one point to undefeated Dunbar ended a great run. Time goes by and clouds one's memories, but the TC experience remains strong. One of my students intro-duced me to her cousin who later became my wife. After my first year there, I bought a new Chevy convertible. Despite our success I never received a raise from Monsignor Nelligan throughout my tenure at Towson Catholic. What a lesson in life that was? Still, to this day, nary a year goes by without my encountering a TC alum with a gleam and remembrance of those great times.

The 1961-62 Towson Catholic Owls, Catholic League Champions and Alhambra Tournament Champions. I'm seated in the center row on the far left.
Photo: Joseph F. Siwak, 1962.

THE ALIENATION OF AFFECTION
How Others See Us

"The fans throughout West Virginia didn't know how to judge the 'hippies' who were giving up their bodies out on the floor."

In 1971 I traveled to Wheeling, West "By God" Virginia to become the athletic director and basketball coach at Wheeling College. The youngest in the Jesuit system, Wheeling was the creation of local Bishop Joseph Hodges, who persuaded the Jesuits with some land and money to "come over the mountain" and start a college in the wilderness of West Virginia – an unlikely place for the Jebbies. Not since Father Marquette did they ever stray too far away from the bright lights.

The "heathens" throughout the State, representing fourteen principalities such as Alderson-Broaddus, Davis & Elkins, Bluefield, and West Liberty had been kicking the crap out of the new Catholic upstart since 1954. The crowds and referees also treated the Cardinals with distance and disdain.

I succeeded a terrific guy named Joe Blaha who after some early success got tired of fighting the Jesuits (the John Thompson era had not started yet) and resigned. The team was 6-17 the previous season and unfortunately all of the players were returning. However, Joe had recruited character and collectively these young men were coachable. I felt confident enough to tell the players at our first meeting, which took place, interestingly enough, in a chemistry lab, that we would have a winning season.

Through the years I learned that offense wins games. You don't score points for defending well. But, if you can't play defense, you won't win. Defense is the tourniquet that stops the bleeding. No defense and you drown in your own blood.

We would play the very basic defense. Defending the perimeter with man for man principles – principles learned from watching Hank Iba's old Coca-Cola film of the 50's that gave a step-by-step analysis of each fundamental. I then watched Maryland's Bud Milliken coach the Iba way, and spent time with Pete Newell the California coach who led our 1960 Olympic Team and later became Bobby Knight's guru. And, as a player with limited ability I did the only thing of which I was capable; stalking my opponent to distraction by denying him access to catch the ball for as long as possible.

The Iba defense consists of strong pressure at the point of the ball when it enters the scoring area, about 22-feet out. The ballhandler is influenced to a point off-center and the first available receiver is denied access to receive the pass, while the other three defenders maintain a position between their man and the ball. The more pressure on the ball, the farther away the defensive players can slide from their men to clog up the lane. It is a man-for-man defense with zone principles. Performed in a limited area it can suffocate the offense, causing turnovers and poor shots. This defense can be successful with limited talent. It is militaristic in nature, fostering cooperation, discipline, selflessness, pride, *espirit de corps*, and survival. The defense is primal. It's the caveman protecting his fire, an animal protecting its young and the militia quelling an invasion.

Players dive on the floor for loose balls, fight through screens, deny cuts to the ball, contest shots, block out, help and recover, knock the ball loose, rebound the missed shot, and effectively assert their manhood with reckless abandon.

The signature move that is the hallmark of this defense is "taking the charge". The defender gives up his body by legally placing himself in the path of the opponent who is usually dribbling or in some cases cutting without the ball. These head on collisions are legal, and produce a foul on the offensive player if the defender has both feet planted on the floor prior to impact. This ultimate act of selflessness fires up the entire team and the crowd. It causes a change in possession and gives the team an emotional lift. When one player consistently takes a charge it becomes contagious.

All our players bought into the system and, with the same crew that went 6-17 the year before, we turned it around to 17-11. It was a memorable year. Vietnam was still playing out and our players were wearing long hair just like the other students. The fans throughout West Virginia did not know how to judge 'hippies' who were giving up their bodies out on the floor. We were a team that got "boos, then cheers" in the same game.

One of our leading spirits was Pat "Spike" McCune from

The 1971-72 Wheeling College Cardinals – a.k.a. the traveling company of "Hair".
Photo: Courtesy of Wheeling Jesuit University.

the up-river steel town of Weirton. He was constantly giving himself up for the team. When he graduated our program was underway. We were getting good players and becoming a contender. Spike stayed on as an admissions counselor and freshman basketball coach. He taught the Iba method with the same passion that he played it.

In the meantime, with better players, I began to open up our offense and overall style of play. The Iba principles were not compatible with our talent and yet, we needed a tourniquet – one that allows you to breathe and move. The answer was the Jack Ramsey Press. Instead of defending the perimeter, Dr. Jack, who won big at tiny St. Joseph's and went on to win a NBA Championship with Portland, setting up "pockets of pressure" all over the floor, goading and harassing opponents into bad decisions by taking calculated risks. The press aligns itself in a 3-1-1 formation and can attack from full, 3/4 and 1/2 court. The passing lanes available to the opponents could be lengthened or shortened by the dictates of the defense. This open court style promotes fast breaking basketball. We did it well, averaging over 90 points per contest and winning 47 games in two years.

Our program helped put Wheeling College on the map, not only throughout the State, but in bigger venues. During my time there we played some of the big boys – Duquesne, Georgetown, Pitt, St. Peter's, South Carolina, and Xavier.

Before Pat moved on, we had a falling out. He didn't take kindly to the wide open style that gave up so many points and he wasn't too enamored with the cavalier attitudes of some of the new recruits. He must have wondered what happened to the fiery coach he met in the chemistry lab a few years back. I had brought out the best in him and now it wasn't good enough. I guess he had the right.

Overall it was a good run, eight years of winning basketball and lots of good memories. And speaking of memories, every time I see a player take a charge, I immediately think of Spike McCune with fondness. Trouble is, because of the modern game, the memories are few and far between.

*AUTHOR'S NOTE: In 1987 Wheeling College changed its name to Wheeling Jesuit College. In 1996 the name was changed once again to Wheeling Jesuit University.

IN THE LION'S DEN
Playing on The Road

"From 1972 to 1979 we visited Xavier seven consecutive times, losing by scores of 91-56, 75-72, 70-66, 95-73, 70-66, and 72-68 in OT in the first six tries. Year seven would be different."

Between the time Big Jim McCafferty's team won the then prestigious NIT title in 1958 and the arrival of the precocious red haired magpie Peter Gillen in 1985, basketball successes at Xavier were few and far between.

The Cincinnati Jesuit institution always had a solid hoops reputation, but our story concerns the "few and far between" era.

Upon being named head coach and athletic director at tiny (600 students) Wheeling College (WV), I took stock of the woeful situation. The Cardinals had no players and no identity. Step one would be to tell them they could succeed; step two, travel by bus instead of rental cars; and step three, upgrade the schedule. Step three was easy. In the early 70's major colleges were in the business of "buying wins." Small, easily beatable schools would come forth for $500 to $1,500 to play a Division I power. It was always away, in the Lion's Den.

These sacrificial blowouts would help shoulder small budgets. The annual flogging paid for the charter buses, put our name out in public, and helped in recruiting. During my fourteen years as a college head coach, I truly came to realize the real meaning of the term "sacrificial lamb."

These games always had a disruptive effect on our teams. If you got crushed, no matter how predictable, it was a blow to one's self esteem. The jeering fans to whom there was no recourse placed the players' emotional well being on the line. I looked at these games as a big challenge, an opportunity for growth, always hoping to come away with a positive. But whenever we lost big, it affected the players adversely for the next few games. When we played well or won, it only inflamed our league peers to get up for us.

Anyway you cut it, it was a bumpy ride. If we were hopelessly down at halftime, we always made a pact to win the second half. There were always goals. We planned to disrupt the hell out of our hosts; hold the ball, press, foul, sub on every dead ball. We used our entire roster in these games. Everyone felt the togetherness that we needed. Seeking respect, we would not go down easy. Each guy played up a notch. These were games to remember – benchmark, tell your kids about, games.

Usually smaller, we used the matchups to tailor a game plan; have our 6'4" center play guard on offense, controlling the tempo as their 6'9" geekster played him loose, or use five guards at once. We were a sting operation. Usually the hosts didn't want to be there. These games were often in between conference games. Injured stars didn't play or took it easy. Their coach might reward the sixth man with a start. We definitely had the mental edge.

Our uniforms were always flashy and different, a big contrast to the home team's dress whites. Our roster always had some city kids who were not about to take a beating without a major confrontation. I would always use reverse psychology, telling the local press that we expected to win, citing the home team's apparent weaknesses. The guarantee money allowed us to travel first class, eat steak and wear blazers. We approached our "big time" games in an upbeat manner. I would start off the bus trips with a Knute Rockne speech about our goal for the day, and how our rivals were no better than us. And it was up to us to prove it, the final score notwithstanding. I preached, never backdown, never lose your resolve, and under no circumstances be intimidated.

By game time we were ready for maximum effort. If these games were on the Vegas line, the home team would be anywhere from a 19 to 35 point favorite.

From 1972 to 1979 we visited Xavier seven consecutive years, losing by scores of 91-56, 75-72, 70-66, 95-73, 70-66, and 72-68 in OT in the first six tries. Year seven would be different.

During this time frame Xavier was an independent. Not having a conference affiliation meant that they hired their own officials. Since the dawn of the TV era in college hoops (1980) officiating has become very professional. Referees no longer belong to towns or regions. Nobody gets cheated on the road anymore. But in the 60's and 70's we still had vestiges of the home boy calls. Tay Baker who had been Ed Jucker's number one assistant at Cincinnati during their NCAA title days in 61 and 62 was the Xavier coach. Well respected, he never made it as a head coach. Their struggling program always "bought" a half dozen wins each year and backed it up with some local refs. Household names such as Aquinas, Thomas More, Centre, Campbellsville, Berea, Union and of course, Wheeling dotted their otherwise prestigious schedule.

In 1977 Tay Baker had two officials who looked like very advanced senior citizens, working the game. It also struck me as unusual that both of these gentlemen were from Hamilton, Ohio. Tay Baker also hails from Hamilton, Ohio.

Soon after the game started it became apparent that we could not win the contest. The playing court was heavily tilted in the Musketeers' favor. These two guys weren't even subtle about it. Our entreaties were handled with disdain and a lack of respect. Our players were distracted and we were being blown out. I looked over to Big Jim McCafferty, the respected ex-coach and athletic director, made eye contact, and in my best sign language told him I didn't abide by these conditions. After his sheepish shrug I called time out.

From that point on we stopped arguing and began to concentrate on playing. On every dead ball for the rest of the first half and into the second half, we substituted five players. This constant flow of troops brought the game to a standstill on every whistle. The Xavier players started to get very angry. Their fans threw objects onto the floor. Tay Baker and Big Jim huddled with their Hessians to check the legality of our actions. Of course no rules were violated. This "ridiculous carnival" was our only legal recourse. It was something like a prison hunger strike, or a 60's sit-in. The ploy succeeded and we rallied to close at 70-66. The game stretched out so long it missed the 11 o'clock news coverage. Afterward I warned Big Jim that we wouldn't be back if the Hamilton gray-beards were again working.

The following year things got worse. We were up one point at halftime. With one second on the clock in front of our bench, Gary Muncie, a flaunting big timer from Ft. Wayne, Indiana called a crunching charge on a Xavier guard who pancaked our guy. The call was made late and reluctantly, only after our entreaties. That was the only Xavier foul of the half. It ruined Muncie's shutout. After calling it he warned me in no uncertain terms. So on the way to the locker room he hits me with two T's (In those days, two technicals on a coach were not an automatic ejection). Big Jim comes in and tries to play the peacemaker. Muncie and his shutout partner are talking ejection, forfeit, etc.

Our players have seen the entire scenario. We had played a great half of basketball despite the unbalanced circumstances. Walking down the runway I told our players to get dressed and formally announced to Big Jim that, "we were leaving." For a moment the players thought I was serious, and, as Big Jim was poised at our locker room door, he heard my instructions. "Boys, we're up one. Let's leave with a victory." "Yeah," they replied. "We're only going to get screwed worse in the second half." I instructed our manager to have the bus driver warm up the bus. Then we sat in perfect silence. Big Jim knocked and knocked again. "Paul, this will ruin your reputation." "What reputation?" I replied. Jim continued, "the national wire services will pick this up, it will be terrible." The players were all stifling their laughter when Big Jim said, "Paul, there is a $1,500 check out here with Wheeling's name on it. You need the money." "Not that bad," I said. "Paul, please be reasonable," he pleaded. "Well O.K. Jim," I relented. "Slide the check under the door please."

Slowly but surely the edge of the white envelope appeared under the door. I told the guys that I wished I could cut it up 15 ways. We laughed, went back out and, after Xavier started the second half shooting four technicals, we lost in OT 72-68.

The local papers highlighted how Wheeling's coach lost the game for his team. But somehow we knew differently. And next season the tide would turn. Justice would be served. It was Tay Baker's last year and the Musketeers were playing hard. They had beaten Southern Cal and Tennessee, and the week before our game, extended Number one ranked Notre Dame. Coming into town I didn't want to be shy, so I told the press, "I'm sick and tired of coming close against Xavier. This year we're going to win." Our players were ready. We pressed them hard, then backed off, and subbed by the numbers, never letting them get comfortable or too far ahead. The game was officiated by Roger Paramore and Randy Drury, two young Mid-American Conference guys who really didn't care who won. With about three minutes to play we caught them, and with 30-seconds left and a 69-68 lead, Xavier turned it over. We worked the clock down to 10-seconds and called time. Our guys were nervous, but it was a good nervous. Not having a "special play" – the kind that never work anyway – I put in our four best shooters along with Gus Harkins, our steadiest ball handler. I was laughing and smiling, cutting the tension. "Just work it around and the first guy who feels it, takes it. It's gonna be a great ride home," I declared.

After two quick passes, Gus reversed the ball to James Ferguson coming to the top of the circle. He caught it, and without a dribble unleashed a picture perfect "J", just like in the finale of the movie "Hoosiers" – Wheeling 70, Xavier 69.

"These were games to remember, benchmark, tell your kids about games."

The following is an account, as it appeared in the Wheeling News-Register, of the 1979 Wheeling College-Xavier basketball game. The article, entitled "The Cardinals' Big Night," appeared on February 11, 1979 and was written by Pat Hanna.

> *It was nearing 4 a.m., Thursday, Feb. 8, at Howard Johnson's Restaurant, National Road, Wheeling. Paul Baker, Wheeling College basketball coach, had just finished an English muffin and a glass of orange drink and was working on his second cup of coffee. Just over six hours earlier, in Cincinnati, Baker had coached his Cardinals to a thrilling one-point win over Xavier University, a major college team which had given top ranked Notre Dame a scare six days earlier. Few small*

college coaches ever get the chance to knock off a major college team; even fewer succeed. Baker was savoring the big triumph; sleep would come later.

It had all begun at 10 a.m., Wednesday, Feb. 7, at the Wheeling College fieldhouse. Members of the men's and women's teams started arriving for the trip to Cincinnati, normally a four-hour ride on Interstate 70 west to Columbus, then Interstate 71 south to Cincinnati. The players milled around, making last minute checks to see if they had packed all of their equipment. It was snowing. Perhaps two inches had fallen since 7 o'clock.

The bus arrived and the equipment was loaded. Sack lunches had been prepared. The traveling party would eat along the way. Players, coaches and others boarded. Baker, his unshaven face casting a 5 o'clock shadow, was the last one on.

"How are the roads?" Baker asked the driver, Chris Schenerlein of Wheeling.

"They're not bad now, but we're supposed to get more snow," Schenerlein replied. "But we've got a good bus. I looked 'em all over this morning and we got the one with the best tires."

The bus pulled out from the fieldhouse parking lot. The players settled back into their seats. Baker reached into a paper sack and pulled out a cigar. Bus trips are not strange to a basketball coach.

"I've lived on these things for 14 years now," Baker said as he lit up his stogie.

The bus departed Wheeling. Through the tunnel, over the Fort Henry Bridge, across Belmont County. Baker opened his briefcase and pulled out a stack of papers – profiles compiled by the highly respected Howie Garfinkel and a dated resume written to NBA clubs by Baker several years ago for a player he coached at the University of Baltimore – Isaiah "Bunny" Wilson, now the women's coach at Wheeling and an assistant to Baker.

169

Baker regards Garfinkel as THE authority on high
school basketball prospects. Garfinkel's Five Star
basketball camp is the hotbed of schoolboy basketball talent, and collegiate coaches throughout the
country subscribe to his service.

"It used to be that Garfinkel would mail information to subscribers on high school players," said
Baker. "Now, you pay a fee for telephone consulta-
tions."

The resume Baker wrote for Wilson didn't go for
naught. Wilson was drafted by the Detroit Pistons
and later played in the now defunct ABA with
Memphis.

Baker chuckled for a moment. "I wonder if Bunny
has ever seen this resume. I don't think he has."
Baker took the resume back to Wilson and returned
to his seat at the front of the bus. "No, he hadn't seen
it."

----

*It was 12 noon. The bus was 30 minutes or so this side
of Columbus. The road was wet and snow covered in
spots, and ice was sticking to the wiper blades, slightly
obscuring vision. But so far, no major problems. "It's
time to eat," came a female's voice from the back of the bus.
Baker got up, turned and flashed a big smile. Laughter
filled the bus. "Our hostess (who turned out to be the student sports information director Judy Freshwater) will
now serve you," Baker said.*

There was enough to feed an army. Each sack was
filled with two ham and Swiss cheese sandwiches,
potato chips, cookies, an apple and a soft drink.

When it's time to eat, it's not time to talk, and
silence prevailed for a few minutes. But once the
food disappeared, Baker began talking again about
his favorite subject – basketball.

Baker had made six pervious trips to Xavier and
had returned to Wheeling each time with a loss. He

had come close five of the six times, but each time Xavier managed to win. Some strange things occurred in previous games. Baker laughed as he recalled some of them. It was as if someone had come up to him in the final minutes and said, "All right, you guys have had your fun, but the party's over now. You're a small college team, and Xavier is a major college team. And it wouldn't look good if you guys beat Xavier right here on their home court, would it?"

Baker revealed his strategy for Xavier. He realized that talent-wise, Xavier was better. After all, a major college team has a much more liberal recruiting budget than does a small college squad. So the Cardinals' upset hopes rested on other things. Baker planned to confuse and rattle the Musketeers with multiple defenses and multiple situations. Baker put together a "kamikaze" squad, a five-man unit which would go onto the court, perhaps for no longer than a minute, in an effort to force a turnover or a bad shot. To win, Baker knew that he would have to call on every bit of coaching knowledge he possessed.

The bus reached the Columbus bypass and headed south on I-71. Cincinnati was another two hours away. Baker decided to get some sleep. "Chris," he said, getting the attention of the bus driver, "we're going to stop at the Holiday Inn-Northeast (of Cincinnati) so the players can rest for a couple of hours before the game. Are you familiar with that area?" The driver nodded affirmatively. Baker dozed off.

On to Cincinnati the bus rolled. Seated in the second row of seats on the right side, directly behind Baker, was Dr. Henry Sutherland, a Wheeling College language professor and the Cardinals' No. 1 fan. "Doc" was celebrating his birthday Wednesday with his favorite people – Baker and the players. Counting the Xavier contest, Sutherland has seen

143 consecutive Wheeling College games.

That's not all. He goes to the practices. He attends games elsewhere. On Jan. 29, when the Cards played Alderson-Broaddus at the WC fieldhouse, Sutherland's streak was nearly broken by a faculty meeting. But he made it in time to see the Cards beat the Battlers.

"He's the one who's kept me going," said Baker.

The bus reaches the Holiday Inn, just a few minutes short of 3 o'clock. Baker , who had awakened a few miles back, got on the bus intercom system. "Okay,", he said, "we've reached the motel. I want the girls to go directly to the restaurant. Your pre-game meal is ready now. After you've eaten, come back to the bus and the driver will take you on to Xavier. We've got some rooms for the guys. Get some rest and report to the restaurant at 4. The bus driver will come back here, and we'll leave for Xavier at 6."

Once inside, Baker passed out room keys to the players. He then went to the restaurant to make sure everything was running smoothly. He sat down, ordered coffee and once again started talking basketball.

The girls and their coach, Wilson, went to the salad bar before the main course was served. One of the women players, Karen Kanick, a freshman from Benwood, came up to the table where Baker and myself were seated.

"I'll have some quotes for you after our game," she said.

The main course was served. One of the girls interrupted Baker's basketball conversation.

"Coach Baker," she said, "what is this? It looks like meat loaf with spaghetti sauce over it."

"It's Salisbury steak," Baker assured her.

The girls got ready to leave for Xavier. Baker wished them, and Wilson, the best of luck. Before

172

going to his room, Baker went up to the chef.

"The men will be in at 4," he said. "Could you go a little easy on the sauce?"

While reading a Cincinnati paper, Baker learned the men's game was set for 7:30 instead of the 8 o'clock starting time he had based pre-game activity around. But he still felt there was ample time in which to prepare. He went to his room and turned on the television. He read some more from the paper. At 4 o'clock, he returned to the restaurant as his players downed their pre-game meal. He then met them to go over the game plan. At 5:15, he returned to his room, showered, shaved and dressed for the game. It was past six o'clock when the players gathered in the lobby for the short trip to the Xavier campus. "Some crazy things happen when we play Xavier," said Cardinal forward Paul Mulholland.

The players boarded the bus. Baker looked at his watch, which read 6:30. "What is it to Xavier, about 15 minutes?" he asked Chris, the driver.

"Maybe not quite that long," replied Schenerlein, "depending on the traffic."

"We're going to be late," Baker said as he turned to "Doc" Sutherland.

"No. Maybe not," Sutherland answered.

"But we've got to be on the floor at seven," Baker came back.

"Well its 6:30 now," Sutherland countered. "If we get there at 15 til, that will give us 15 minutes to dress."

The bus arrived at Schmidt Memorial Fieldhouse. The players went directly to the locker room. Inside hangs a banner which reads, "Xavier University 1958 NIT Champion." Just after 7, Xavier took the floor. It was 7:10 when the Cards came out. The WC women had lost to the Xavier women, 81-74, after leading by three at the half. Wilson joined Baker on the bench. The Cards were in their traveling gold jerseys. Eddie Graham wore black sneakers; the rest of the players were in white. The National Anthem was played. It was time to play ball.

Xavier took a 2-0 lead, but the Cardinals came back and took a 10-point advantage with 14:07 left in the first half. At 13:07 and again at 11:59, Baker put his "kamikaze" squad onto the floor. At 11:11 he did the same thing, but there was a problem. Mike Joseph was wearing jersey No. 23, but the official scorebook had him with No. 11. Joseph usually wears No. 11, but that particular jersey had been stolen a few days earlier from the WC fieldhouse. The change wasn't made in the scorebook. An automatic technical foul resulted, and Baker was furious.

"Do I have to do everything myself?" he screamed.

The first half was close. A last second basket gave the Musketeers a 32-30 halftime lead.

Xavier assumed control in the second half. The Musketeers led, 66-57, with 4:59 to go, and it looked as if Baker was going to lose to Xavier for the seventh time.

But the Cards came back. A basket by James Ferguson with 38 seconds left cut the Xavier lead to one, 69-68. The Musketeers then lost the ball to give WC a chance to win it. With four seconds remaining, Ferguson hit a 22-foot jumper. The Cardinals had done it. Baker and Wilson embraced in front of the WC bench.

Inside the victorious Cardinal dressing room, there was jubilation, hugging, hand-slapping and cheers. The Lord's Prayer was said. Baker happily answered the questions of reporters, including two youngsters who were covering the game for their school paper in Hamilton, Ohio. On his way out of the fieldhouse, Baker picked up a piece of paper. Once on the bus, he looked at it and found the words of the Xavier alma mater. He began singing. Many on the bus began searching for something to place over their ears.

The bus stopped at a McDonald's just outside Cincinnati. Baker passed out the meal money. The players ate, still savoring their big win. Karen Kanick came up with a quote.

"I took one shot," she said. "Can I get my name in the paper?"

The bus then headed north on I-71. The radio was turned on, and tunes like Al Stewart's "The year of the Cat" and "Shake Your Bootey" blared over the speakers.

Baker fired up a victory cigar.

"This one's been a long time coming," he said.

The traveling party sang "Happy Birthday" to "Doc" Sutherland. Baker tested his voice once again.

At the conclusion, Sutherland rose and said, "I'm happy."

Most of the players slept on the way back. Baker also cat-napped, but his main dream that night had become a reality a couple of hours earlier. Cardinal guard Gus Harkins couldn't sleep. He came up to the front of the bus, pulled out a jump seat and began rapping with the bus driver. On I-70 near Cambridge, the bus hit what felt like a crater. If that didn't awaken the players, the Fort Henry Bridge did.

Baker sat at Howard Johnson's. He was still talking basketball at 4 a.m. He looked at his watch. "Well, it began at 10 o'clock this morning. That's an 18-hour day." And he enjoyed every minute of it.

TAKING A BACK SEAT
Captain Bligh Traveling in Steerage

"If you ever want to find out how your family would do if you were gone, take a back seat and keep quiet."

Stretching over two decades I commanded the wheel of the family station wagon on countless vacation and holiday trips. Mom and the three kids, luggage, gifts, toys, food-stuffs, and an occasional pet were all under my control as I tempted the fates of the highway. Being an athletic coach, action and firm decision making became my right. I called the shots. The route, the stops, length of stops, what and when to eat, fast pace, slow pace, pass, and the changing of lanes were all at my discretion. Whether I was disciplining the kids or arguing with mom, we drove ever onward regardless of the pitfalls. I was Captain Bligh of the Vista Cruiser.

Now the trips have stopped. The kids have grown and we moved back home, eliminating the need for family visits. The station wagon era has passed, and just in time, as a three hour stint behind the wheel now brings yawns of impending sleep.

Those days were wild. I don't know how we survived. My only instincts were to get us there and back in one piece.

It's not how you played the game but whether you won. We won but what a price. Mom and the kids still refer to the Captain Bligh era with a chuckle and many a disparaging remark. As the children began to drive and mom became more independent, any and all trips would begin with my being relegated to the back seat. Who ever heard of Captain Bligh traveling in steerage?

I will always remember our last family trip. We were taking our youngest son Nicholas to lacrosse camp, some three hours away. His ground rules: "Mom drives and pop sits in the back or I don't go." We all must suffer for sins of the past. For the first time in the three year history of my new car, I climbed into the back seat, along with luggage, one pillow, a bag of snacks and a deflated ego.

There was no glass plate separating us, but for all that I was recognized, it surely could have been. Their conversation was live and animated as mom sped down the highway in my car. I grabbed bits and pieces of their words, but the back speaker blared into my ears, further disorienting me. I decided just to watch. Mom's profile still showed a youthful cast and young Tarzan's legs propped up on the dashboard were hairier than mine. They did acknowledge me as the snacks were demanded. They began to play 20 Questions and I tried to listen through the loud music. They were having a great time and even seemed to know where they were going. Mom didn't need instructions on when to change lanes, or where to stop, or what route to take. Nicky called the shots on changing stations, snacks, and pit stops. They didn't know I existed. It was as if a cloud were over me and I floated timelessly in space. Captain Bligh had turned into Carousel's Billy Bigelow. I felt better when they acknowledged me, even though the remarks concerned buckling up and to not eat all of the snacks.

Later mom asked me about the turnpike exit. Ah, control

restored. Before I could shout the command, her youngest son calmly gave her the needed information as she nimbly flicked on the blinker and moved into the exit ramp. As we entered the town the directions to the campus became intricate. I was asked to participate. With an opportunity to again join the family, I couldn't blow it. I calmly discussed each turn and option – no commands, no declarations, and no "I told you so's." They made it. We got out of the car. No one was sweaty and no one was disheveled. No one was mad and no one was tired.

If you ever want to find out how your family would do if you were gone, take a back seat and keep quiet. You will learn a lot. I rather liked the trip.

Signed, Captain Bligh – H.M.S. Vista Cruiser, Ret.

LET'S PLAY TWO

A Zany Bus Trip to West Virginia

"Two hours into our adventure, somewhere near the Shenandoah River Bridge, yours truly hits an ace-deuce for $360. . ."

Coaching basketball at Baltimore University was difficult. With no dining hall or dormitories available, we had little to offer out of state kids, other than a chance to play. The local talent was thin and the good ones went away to school.

But baseball was different. The local kids were good and plentiful. Even the second liners could play on a collegiate level. The two years I managed we won championships despite the coaching. The guys were talented and loose, and after arduous winters on the basketball court, I was also loose. It made for great player-coach relationships.

Every Saturday of the Spring semester we would play double-headers as we cut a swath through the Mason Dixon Conference. The home games were family affairs with parents, friends, and fans coming out to our Rogers Avenue diamond, one of the city's best.

It was the road trips, however, where the sparks would fly. One trip of particular note was a visit to Shepherd College in the West Virginia panhandle. In those days,

181

Shepherd was a cow-college and its baseball diamond was actually a converted cow pasture. The outfield grass was ankle deep. We could beat Shepherd with our eyes closed and, since we were tied for first place with Towson State, we decided to leave Jack Hubbard, our assistant coach, home to watch and report on Towson's double-header with Hampden-Sydney College. We knew we would sweep Shepherd and if Hampden-Sydney won just one game, we would be champs.

At 9:00 a.m. the Hartford Motor Coach "Silver Bullet" pulled up to the Rogers Avenue Fieldhouse. George Dodson was our personal driver. He was a wonderful fellow who loved making these trips and he always avoided the pot-holes. Shortly thereafter, my Bees began to show up. From all over Baltimore they came. The East Baltimore guys brought two trash cans filled with iced cold beverages. The Pig Town boys brought three dozen corn beef sandwiches and the Italians brought several cases of produce. We were preparing to "play two." These were all working class Baltimore kids who played ball, went to school, and some-how managed to hold a part-time job.

No sooner had the bus departed, everybody pulled out their money – large wads in small bills. Two games of "in-between" got underway, one for lower stakes in the front of the bus and a high stakes game in the back. Players would alternate between games depending on how their luck was running. Playing cards, and eating sandwiches on the way to "play two" was heaven to these young urchins who were struggling with the travails of college during the week.

To the uninitiated, "in-between", also known as "match the pot," is a game where the dealer rips out two cards. The next player then has the option of betting whether the next card will fit "in-between" the two cards. The best hand is an ace-deuce. A likely winner, the player bets or matches the pot, that the next card will fall "in between" the ace and deuce. If an ace or a deuce comes up, the player then has to pay the pot. When cards like 10 and 7 come up, whoever has that turn, simply passes. When a player matches the pot and loses, the bus erupts.

Money, food and good fellowship were flying through the "Silver Bullet" on this sunny Saturday morning as we headed into West "By God" Virginia. Chants of "build-the-pot, build-the-pot" are echoed every time a loser throws down his money. Two hours into our adventure, somewhere near the Shenandoah River bridge, yours truly hits an ace-deuce for $360, effectively breaking the bank for the day. The hit is met with exultation and then mumbling and groaning. This was Atlantic City for these guys, thirty years before the fact.

As lunch is being served, I begin thinking baseball. Two things are certain – we sweep easily and everybody plays. Then, with the euphoria of the $360 hit, a brain-storm rises. Everybody's name goes into a hat and, randomly, I select a name and write it onto the lineup card. Our left-handed first-baseman started at shortstop, the relief pitcher was the catcher and so on. Today, every baseball player's dreams would be fulfilled as we would let everyone, except our pitchers, pitch at least one inning. In keeping with the day, a pool was formed for the one who pitched the best inning.

As we pulled onto the Shepherd campus, George wheeled the bus right onto the first base side of the cow pasture. We toyed with the Rams "baseball" team. The players used their private charter as a refreshment stand/dugout. George kept the air conditioning running and everybody was loosy goosy, winning the opener 13-5. Between games the Shepherd players and the umpires – the notorious

Lightner Brothers known as "Hook & Crook" – came over for some liquid refreshment. The highlight of the first game was an inside the park home run to short right center, as the Shepherd outfielders couldn't find the ball.

Midway through the second game, George pulled the Silver Bullet back onto the road so he and I could motor up to a phone booth (no cell phones existed in those days). I dialed the number of a Towson convenience store where Hubbard answered and informed me that Towson State had lost their first game – we were the champs. Rolling back down to the field, the bus was met by our entire team and all the players gathered around as George ceremoniously hand-ed me an envelope. I read slowly, "Towson State 6," fol-lowed by a long hesitation, "Hampden-Sydney 7." A rous-ing cheer broke loose. Shepherd was dispatched, we show-ered in their gym and prepared to head home.

I still had $360 cash in my pocket, a lot of money in 1968. The money really belonged to the players. After all, they brought the food and won the title. While they finished their showers, George and I mapped out the return trip. I called ahead and got complimentary passes to the Clubhouse at the Shenandoah Race Track. As each player stepped off the bus he got a twenty. For the NCAA's benefit, it was meal money. We had a great time, staying for all nine races and being introduced as the Mason Dixon Champions and guests of the track management.

By the time we reached the Rogers Avenue parking lot some 15 hours later, no one was broke, and we were champi-ons. Ernie Banks coined the phrase, but the Baltimore Bees, on this day, put real meaning to the phrase, "Let's play two."

SHOE CAPERS
Should I or Shouldn't I?

"With all the stripes, buckles, pads, colors and surreal sur-
faces, they looked like studio props from an old Buck Rogers
flick."

Recently I went into a sporting goods store to purchase a
pair of walking shoes. Propped on a little wall with
pedestals were dozens upon dozens of today's modern
sports shoes. There were shoes for walking, running, jogging, and playing every sport imaginable. They dared your
eyes to look away as their color and style magnetized you to
the wall. With all the stripes, buckles, pads, colors and surreal surfaces, they looked like studio props from an old Buck
Rogers flick.

Foreboding, thick and heavy looking, they are actually as
light as a feather – much like icing on a cake. The Nike corporation and her competing corporate giants are battling
hard for market share. The more categories they create, the
more models they can produce, and the more sales they can
generate. The brogans are "fashion statements" first and per-
formance driven second. Gazing at this 21st Century collection of pop art, even a compulsive buyer like myself couldn't
pull the trigger. I walked away feeling relieved. The Battle

Star Galactica collection belongs to the younger set.

My experience with athletic shoes goes back to the late 40's when Spot Bilt made a great shoe of soft pliable black leather. Their trademark was a round white plastic tab on the back of the shoe. They had removable cleats and came in low and high cut models. The only fashion statement was when some guys wore them with white shoe laces.

All the running backs on our high school team wore Spot Bilts and during my senior year I was locked in a hopeless struggle for the starting left halfback spot. Jerry was bigger and faster, but I was quick and tough. Our coach preached toughness, yet he started Jerry over me. In final analysis, they go for speed over attitude – even ex-Knute Rockne coal miners. Don't let them tell you any different.

After the first two games, I played only briefly despite Jerry's lackluster performances and I couldn't stand it. Thus, I decided to take matters into my own hands.

Prior to our next game, a Friday contest against Poly in Memorial Stadium, the players packed their uniforms and equipment into canvas duffel bags for placement on the school bus, as we always did. I waited until everyone had packed their bags and, with my hands trembling with nervous guilt, I stood all alone among the forty bags. I pondered, "Should I or shouldn't I?" Should I won out.

Stumbling over the baggage I arrived at Jerry's locker and, reaching down into his bag, I felt his shoes with the laces tied in a knot. They were Spot Bilt high tops. The managers would be arriving soon, so I acted quickly – grabbing the shoes in the eerie silence and, running out into the October dusk, boomeranging them onto the practice field. That night I dressed quickly, put my helmet on and sat silently at my locker, staring down at my low cut Spot Bilts. I was still on edge fighting guilt and shame, while across the room Jerry stood in full uniform with no shoes. I kept my head down, knowing if our eyes ever met I could be exposed. Running onto the field I saw Coach Vic Wojcihovski and Brother Ricardus huddled in conference. They dispatched a manager in a taxi cab to get Jerry some shoes. That made my guilt disappear. I had at least an hour.

Poly was big and strong. Still shaking like a leaf, I returned the opening kick to midfield and for the remainder of the season, Jerry and I alternated at halfback.

Some twenty years later I met Jerry on the Clifton Park Golf Course and confessed.

My devious action gained me a little playing time, but a similar act paid even greater dividends for one old pro.

Moving into the 1960's basketball footwear was rapidly changing. Shoes were no longer canvas. The Converse monopoly with their famous Chuck Taylor model was about to end. Back in 1963 I hosted a basketball clinic and the famous St. John's mentor Joe Lapchick was our featured speaker. He was the star center of Nat Holman's famous Original Celtics – the Bill Russell of his day. By his own admission, Joe, the son of Eastern European immigrants, never got past the fifth grade. One day he got a letter from the Converse Rubber Company. Struggling to read the fancy letter, he gave up and tossed it into the waste basket. Spying the disposed missive, a lowly substitute waited until the locker room was empty (shades of yours truly), retrieved the letter and sent a reply to Converse. It signaled the beginning of a beautiful relationship. His name, Chuck Taylor.

At Wheeling College in the 70's we were trying to become a real basketball school, actually buying shoes for our players. We used the Converse Shoe bank, buying in bulk from the Converse rep in Pittsburgh. We were hard pressed but bought two pairs of white leather Cons for each player. As the season wore on some of the starters were into their second pair. The little used subs were still on their first pair. Big

Bob, a 6'-8" sub with size 15's, blew out his heel in a late season practice. When I went to the shoe supply, his back ups had been used for a front line player. There were no leather 15's in stock at the local dealers, so we got Bob a new pair of canvas Chuck Taylor high tops to finish the season. Upon seeing the canvas shoes he launched into a wounded tirade and told me in no uncertain terms where I could put the shoes. At that time I ended his dubious career.

A few nights later at a home game, right after the National Anthem, Bob's fraternity brothers unleashed a torrent of assorted shoes onto the court. Even in those days shoes were a fashion statement.

With all due respect to the memory of the Original Celtic legend, "Lapchick's" might not have caught on.

FIRE & BRIMSTONE
A Language Within A Language

"Every halftime I would deliver a tirade aimed at their manhood, replete with the standard expletives."

Basketball has its own language – a vernacular that embraces all the terms and descriptions to let us understand and appreciate the game. However, the coach has a vernacular of his own, one that sets him apart. It's a language within a language. Gestures, signs, body english, voice patterns, inflections, facial gyrations, sitting, standing, pacing and jumping are manifestations of a coach's persona. These guys become a game within a game. Fans love to watch animated coaches.

When a coach brings words and phrases not found in Webster's, he brings added fire to an already volatile scene. This "Fire & Brimstone" can make or break a team fast. As the game's fast pace moves on to the tune of cheering crowds, whistle tooting refs and clipboard waving assistants, communication is difficult – especially on the road. Can the players actually communicate with the coach? Yes, but only with great difficulty.

The better a team is taught in practice, the less they need to be counseled during the game. Timeouts are the respite needed to impart knowledge. The halftime talk usually resolves the first half and points the team in a winning direction for the final push.

In the large arenas it is difficult to hear the coach's running dialogue unless you are seated close behind the bench. In the smaller venues where there is limited seating and small crowds, you can hear the entire banter. No one can hear the halftime talk, but you can imagine what each coach is like based on what you hear in open court.

Duke never plays before less than 5,000 fans and it is always loud. You cannot hear Coach Krzyzewski deliver his "Fire and Brimstone", but if you are a good lip reader you get the drift. When I coached at the University of Baltimore, my style made Earl Weaver look like an altar boy. And, when we played a game in front of 163 fans and the visiting team's bus driver, everybody heard my words, including our University President. But "Fire and Brimstone" comes with basketball – for better or worse. With all the major problems today, it is really a Venial sin, part of the morality play that is unfolding in front of us; good vs. evil, political refs, partisan fans, posturing players, and single minded coaches. It's part of the script.

My sons grew up "on the bench" at Wheeling College. They collected warmups, gave out towels and water bottles, and listened to their father speak the vernacular of the profession. I became aware of this situation and it did trouble me. Jo Jo Retton rationalized his actions by telling his children, "this is part of daddy's job". By using "Fire and Brimstone" you are sending a message to your team. Each player makes his own value judgement based on his upbringing. What kind of man is our coach? Is this just the tip of the iceberg of an immoral man? Are we in the presence of a potential mass murder, or is it a manifestation of a fiery temper and nothing more? They all have a different slant on their coach and, if misunderstood, it can hurt team unity.

One night in Wheeling, against a weak opponent whose coach I had no love for, we were underachieving badly. I left the bench and marched into the locker room, came back out and sat in the stands for the rest of the first half. At halftime I began to blister the starters, telling four of them to perform an impossible act. The fifth starter was Rodney Gaddy, our captain, coach on the floor, money in the bank on the foul line player, and the eventual Valedictorian of his graduating class, as well as a Georgetown Law School Honor Grad. As I paused at the locker room door before I slammed it off its hinges, I turned and told Rodney that he should also do the same thing. We rallied and won. Years later Rodney confided that had I not included him in the tirade, there would have been a huge rift between him and the blistered starters, as they would have viewed him as the coach's pet, thus diminishing his role as a team leader. Fire and Brimstone always has its price.

Many years later I returned to coaching briefly at a small, eclectic, highly academic institution called Park School. Located in Brooklandville, Maryland, the Bruins' basketball program went 0 for the previous year, losing every game on each level. The kids did O.K. in soccer and lacrosse, but the Winter was reserved for field trips, college visits, Caribbean get-aways, internships, and ski weekends. Saturday morning practices were impossible. The administration was oblivious, but I wasn't and my old instincts got the best of me early on. I poured myself into the job, Fire and Brimstone included. It was not pretty as I attempted to get these kids to play basketball. They had no fundamental background or inclination to buy into the program. When prodded to the max they did respond with competitive spirit and pride. The season went something like this: Up 20 at halftime, our opponents would sub early in the second half. We'd press and try to come back. The goal was to steal a few games and not to let them double our score. We won five games. Every halftime I would deliver a tirade aimed at their pride and manhood, replete with the standard expletives. I would make certain that there was eye contact and commitment. The kids secretly enjoyed it and came out smoking in the second half.

One night against the Friends School Quakers we were within striking distance at the half. I was ready for my usual speech. The kids had settled into their seats in the tiny, cramped cracker box locker room. I was down on one knee and it was so quiet you could hear the proverbial pin drop. I heard a noise. Looking at the locker room door to my right I was at eye level with the air vents at the bottom portion of the door. Two slats were missing and, as I peered closer through the openings, I beheld the visage of one "Ace Mallonee," a second grader and the son of lacrosse and soccer coach Lucky Mallonee. Little Ace was sitting Indian style behind the door with his Coke and popcorn waiting for the Fire and Brimstone show. I hesitated for an instant, but the players didn't notice. Flashing through my mind were memories of my young sons at Wheeling College and how they had grown up no worse for their experiences. I unleashed the Fire and Brimstone. After all, I couldn't disappoint Ace, and there were the ominous Friends School Quakers to contend with. Plus, it's only a Venial sin. I hope.

SATURDAY MORNING PRACTICE
The Day A Team Forms Its Persona

"The action is full of tension and accountability. Again, thoroughbreds come to the fore, as the others are carried along in the wake."

Take the opening scene from the movie "Hoosiers" with the multi-colored foliage swirling in the cold Autumn wind and you have basketball in the air. Cold, Fall Saturday mornings beckon players and coaches to practice. The gym is creaking itself alive as the warm air speeds through the aluminum ducts causing noisy upheavals. Chards of warm light stream through the upper windows. The players wander in, coming alive according to the severity of their Friday night activity. Some are animated and energetic, others fight the cold and the early hour. The wise slept ten hours. The foolish will soon pay. The locker room juke box vibrates, players dress, tape and chatter.

Coaches huddle in the cold office over warm coffee and doughnuts, scanning the day's objectives. A manager writes out the practice plan for the players on a chalk board. From the floor comes the first staccato dribble, a cord ripple and voices – all wake up calls. The staff leaves their coffee in mid-gulp as they stride onto the court. The team comes together and the coach speaks his mantra. The morning stretch begins – veterans in the warmth of the sun's glow, rookies on the cool edges.

Saturday is the day teams form their persona. All week long there are classes and time constraints. The world of education rules. But early Saturday morning, when academia is sleeping it off, basketball becomes life itself. Coaches point for Saturday morning practice.

As full court drills heat up, the first drops of sweat bead up on faces and spatter the floor. The staff corrects and instructs on the fly, allowing a rhythm to evolve – a rhythm that runs through good teams. Establish it here and now. Occasionally a door slams, a phone rings, and a horn honks, but the players are oblivious. The coaches move through the practice plan. As defense is stressed shoes squeak out their own concerto, a message that the team is serious. No one dares to ask a question. No one breaks the flow. There will be time for that later – now, only the coach speaks.

The first hour is conditioning and fundamentals at game tempo. Thoroughbreds step up, prospects struggle and suspects emerge. Players take each other's measure. Coaches see all. The pecking order unfolds.

The second hour is cerebral work as the staff puts in a new segment – Zone Defense and Offense – Press Defense and Offense. A part of the team's fabric is sown in place. Here, communication is essential as the team and staff speak to each other in the vernacular of the game – eye contact, gestures, body language, and voice inflections. First we start with a walk through, then half speed, game tempo, then live. Some players execute naturally, others are robotic. Another insight emerges.

The third hour is "scrimmage time". Officials appear. Managers hook up the scoreboard. The gym has totally awakened in a brilliant splash of sun. Together with the overhead lights, everyone is truly under a microscope. Players put on numbered shirts. A 40-minute game situation with stats and film is in the offing. Coaches will look hard for telltale signs of progress. Players have the dual master to serve, team cohesion and playing time. The bright morning is now in full bloom as the scrimmage begins. Familiar faces arrive carrying coffee cups. They sit on the edges, watching their team, making their own assessments. The action is full of tension and accountability. Again, thoroughbreds come to the fore, as the others are carried along in the wake. Everyone gets playing time.

The head coach is busy watching the web of emerging patterns. The assistants are busy coaching the two teams, as he gets a grip on the persona of his team. He catalogs to memory what this team can and cannot do – ditto for the players as individuals. This mental grindstone will repeat itself often. It's a Saturday morning chemistry lab with many

Saturday morning practices at Wheeling College, like this one during my first year with the Cardinals (1971-72), were instrumental in turning around a program which had only won six games in each of the three previous seasons.
Photos: Courtesy of Wheeling Jesuit University.

experiments. The managers total the stats and the tape is prepared.

In the fourth hour it is time for the players to "suffer it up." Twenty minutes of suicide wind sprints, encompassing the entire court in 30-second segments, are the prelude for the trip outside to the running track for the timed mile run. The standard time being six minutes.

It is nearing mid-day as the team enters the locker room. Music blares as they begin to unwind. Loud banter, missing the past hours, fills the air as they critique each other's "*faux pas*" from the morning. Nicknames are born here, as well as life-long friendships. Mutual suffering is the tie that binds. The warm shower is a magic elixir, as they talk with "visions of sugar plumbs" about the coming season. For now, the pressure is off as lunch and college football games await. The last stragglers bang the door.

In a dark room the staff is grinding film.

A WALK IN THE PARK
Golf in The Inner City

"The course itself is indestructible. If it were human it would take on the elements of Carmen Basilio, Chuck Bednarik, and Clint Courtney with a touch of Johnny Unitas thrown in for good measure."

Located nearly in the middle of Baltimore City, Clifton Park is an old public golf course that has seen better days. Inescapably trapped in an urban ghetto for the past quarter century, it continues to survive. Golf starved Baltimore cannot afford to lose another venue. Clifton lies between two major North-South arteries, Harford and Belair Roads. Weaving through the course are over three miles of two way streets, moving thousands of vehicles during the day. In the Southwest corner between the park and the golf course lies a newcomer, less than thirty years old, Lake Clifton Senior High School. Large and overcrowded, the students travel through the course all during the day.

It is a typical muggy Baltimore Summer morning when we tee it up at 7:02. The City is already alive and traffic begins to flow. Coming off number one, the intersection of Harford Road and 32nd Street is choked with cars and pedestrians. As we wait to cross over, an over the shoulder look reveals the glowing sunrise enveloping the downtown skyline as the summer haze begins to burn off. To the left of the flowing traffic, just a par five away, is "The Love Child" – Memorial Stadium – former home of the Colts, Orioles, and now Ravens. It all adds to the rich flavor of Clifton, which, according to its longtime pro, the late Joey Vaeth, has more character than England's fabled St. Andrew's ever had. "That St. Andrews was just Clifton with wind," said Vaeth the Summer before he passed away.

Character aside, the course continues to fight for its survival. In the late 80's, the City of Baltimore turned over its five municipal golf courses, Carroll Park, Clifton Park, Forest Park, Mount Pleasant and Pine Ridge to a corporation formed by then Mayor William Donald Schaefer. The City was losing over a half million dollars per year and the courses were in disarray. This arrangement stopped the bleeding and the project has become a model for other urban venues around the nation. But, in the spring of 1996, Mayor Kurt Schmoke, a native Baltimorean with a Yale pedigree, in dire need of funds, threatened not to renew the pact. Clifton cringed, but cooler heads prevailed as the corporation found a way to donate more funds to the Inner City Children's Recreation project. The win-win situation continued and the Clifton course endured another challenge.

Divesting itself of the distractions, Clifton is still a decent round. A hilly layout with flat greens, it looks easier than it is. Because of the environment it is a mental exercise, which golf is meant to be. It is so easy it's hard.

The course is well maintained. With only a half dozen men working, it is remarkable. There are some well heeled private clubs in the area with more maintenance problems than Clifton. This is particularly true of the greens. They are kept a tad long to absorb the unrelenting Baltimore humidity and the unending tramp tramp of her golfing rabble. The

Joey Vaeth, the Head Pro at Clifton Park Golf Course in the late 80's and the course's longtime Assistant Pro, said his beloved East Baltimore links "had more character" than England's legendary St. Andrew's.
Photo: Courtesy McKeldin Library/University of Maryland – Baltimore News Post/News American collection.

staff goes about its business of keeping the course in shape, ignoring the golfers, as if the course were closed for the day. They are working class people who take pride in their work. Open since 1915, Clifton is sacred ground. Only a snob or someone without a sense of tradition would demean it.

Clifton's current Head Pro is Mark Paolini. Hired in 1989 as her seventh Head Pro, he has all the PGA training and background for the job. However, nothing in PGA school could have prepared him for his daily duties. The previous half century (1935-85) Clifton was run by the fabled Johnny Bass and his able assistant Joe Vaeth, who eventually succeeded him. Old fashioned gentlemen, they promoted the game and not themselves. Bass always wore a shirt and tie and a big smile. Joe carried on the Bass tradition. They were the pioneers of golf in Baltimore and Clifton was the epicenter. Those times are past. No one of material substance frequents Clifton anymore. Yet scores of this areas low handicappers who went on to country club fame cut their golf eye teeth on the Clifton links. Billy Collins was a successful Tour Pro and two-time Ryder Cup member. Dick Mullen along with the Gehring brothers, Paul and Bill, were long time area pros. Eddie Meyer was one of Baltimore's very best amateurs, and Kenny Scales went on to win over a half dozen Country Club of Maryland titles. Sadly, no one came along to replace them.

Now the traffic comes from old-timers. Baltimore born and bred retirees, ranging in their late fifties all the way up to octogenarians, have adopted Clifton as their second home. Walking through the clubhouse I am reminded of those post Depression sporting crowds in old Ebbetts Field. The rest of the players are a public parks melange of assorted hackers. The common man in spades. There are no airs put on at Clifton Park.

The course itself is indestructible. If it were human it

would take on the elements of Carmen Basilio, Chuck Bednarik, and Clint Courtney with a touch of Johnny Unitas thrown in for good measure.

Paolini's pro shop is modest, befitting the clientele. Lessons are few and far between. Mark is the plant manager, traffic cop, trouble shooter, public relations director and bookkeeper. You won't find him in an alpaca sweater and golf slacks as he patrols his "area" in a golf cart. The two way radio is a constant companion. Perched on key knolls and vistas he can see large sections of the course with a sweep of an eye. Calls come in from the clubhouse with questions only he can answer, and from rangers about slow play or neighborhood unrest. The cops and 911 are always in the loop. It is not beneath him to police the area on his rounds, picking up bottles, paper cups and food wrappers. Paolini is in control of his environment. He must deal with the public in the truest sense. No golf professional in America has a more diverse constituency than Mark Paolini.

As I play the course my memories of days gone by in Clifton Park keep coming back. I played sandlot baseball on all of her manicured diamonds in the 50's. The Clifton Relays were a big event for local high school track and field teams and schools came from miles away to compete. Now the fields are in total disarray and the track is nonexistent. Lake Clifton High School built in the 70's is already decaying. And just on the edge of the park on Washington Street was the former row house home of my compare' (my Godfather Vince Dundee) Vince's older brother, Joe Dundee – the old Welterweight Champion of the World. Just about every Baltimore born and bred athlete from days gone by, played in Clifton Park. Though the golf course survives, the rest is history.

Scenes From A Walk In The Park:

* Number one is a 540-yard monster whose fairway dips

over 50 feet below street level as the Harford Road gabled row houses gaze down on the players, who then rise straight uphill to the far off green, the highest point in Baltimore City.

* Number two is a blind downhill short par four. Far on the horizon is the specter of the Francis Scott Key Bridge named after the guy who wrote the National Anthem. On a clear day aim for the middle span.

* On old number three there is a panoramic view of East Baltimore row house rooftops stretching for miles. Back in the 50's, from behind the fence, stood a hot dog stand in a row house yard. Off premise and legal, Baltimorese style. The shack was less than thirty feet from the fringe of the green.

* Number five borders Belair Road, where carts used to motor up to the package stores at the Erdman Avenue intersection for a six pack while waiting to tee off. This action is now prohibited and clearly marked on the scorecard. One day while I was on the tee a fire engine was putting out a row house fire. Amidst the blaring sirens and two police cruisers – not fifty feet away – everyone in my foursome hit straight tee shots.

* A hefty golfer in a tank top with hi-top socks and tennis shoes relieving himself while leaning on a tiny sapling not more than a chip shot off Belair Road.

* Not many years ago, early starting time golfers would encounter curled up homeless types sleeping in sandtraps on cardboard beds.

* Lake Clifton students seeking access to Belair Road and other bus routes would climb the fence bordering old number seven, walking right over the green and down the fairway, stopping all play. Paolini cut a hole in the fence that borders the cemetery, leading to an orderly traffic pattern down the edge of the fairway.

* The clubhouse has a 50's aura. Guys are playing cards

in the middle of the day, talking golf, drinking coffee and kibitzing. The snack bar is also a throwback operation. There is always a guy with a silver pompadour or a gum cracking waitress at your service. The grille is hot and greasy. The food is basic, predictable and good. The prices are in line with the austerity of the customer base, but I have seen guys with shirts and ties come off the street for lunch.

* Out on the course the drinking fountains are Department of Public Works relics circa 1930's and the few public benches are caked with countless coats of cracking green paint.

* Joe Vaeth always said that St. Andrews was a dirt bag, sheep infested mess that they gussied up for tournament time, whereas Clifton was always in a state of playability. "You can have St. Andrews by the sea, I'll take Clifton above the Harbor." Staunchly loyal, Joe was on the course almost until the day he died. His spirit permeates the grounds.

* Playing at Clifton is an adventure. You cross over heavily trafficked streets four times per round. Kids are riding bikes all through the course and roller blading down the dirt cart paths. It is also the natural thoroughfare for foot traffic between Belair and Harford Roads. On five holes you are putting in direct view of motor vehicles. The irreverence of the honking horns and derisive hoots from this "four wheel gallery" can effect your stroke if you let it. The ghetto kids are more respectful. Unless, of course, they decide to rob you. In recent years there have been thefts and hold ups right on the course in broad daylight. It seems to run in streaks, never reaching epidemic proportions. It's the price you pay for continuing to play at Clifton.

* Throughout the course there are kids hawking balls and selling 16-ounce sodas for a buck. Clifton's version of the country club refreshment carts. On number fourteen there is a ramshackle snack bar and bathroom hooked onto an

ancient car barn.

* Unlike most public venues, you can play Clifton in four hours regardless of the time of day.

* Facing Harford Road bordered by 32nd Street is a flat gravel area where Bill Conco parks his car and sets up his mobile golf store. Dozens of putters and woods lean on the side of his car as shiny golf balls, packaged in plastic egg cartons, are displayed on the gravel show room floor. Bill also sells cold sodas. Paolini has no choice in the matter, because Bill, like the old hot dog stand of the 50's, is not on the golf course property.

* Clifton's Pagoda Mansion House – not to be confused with the famous Pagoda House in Patterson Park – built in the late 18th century by Johns Hopkins, who owned the entire tract of land that is Clifton Park, is still standing as one of Baltimore's most lasting landmarks. Hopkins would climb to the top of the tower and check on the clipper ships coming and going from Baltimore Harbor. Now it serves as a line for your drive on eighteen, which is a great finishing hole. The tee is adjacent to the number one green on Baltimore's highest vista. You are looking down a rolling fairway with two large dips. At the base of the second dip, about a hundred yards out are two large trees that straddle each side of the fairway. At 495 yards it is reachable in two but both shots must be very accurate to a narrow green. Behind the green is the Pagoda Mansion House rising. A fitting end to a tradition laden track.

On a Labor Day Weekend following a withering month of Baltimore heat, the course is packed with Clifton's everyday people. The sky is a bright blue with nary a cloud in sight and miraculously the humidity is gone. The fairways are bright green, cutting a swath through the dried out rough. The greens are cut close with nary a brown spot showing. There is an aura of manicured beauty, like an "inner city kid

The magestic skyline of Baltimore's downtown district is clearly visible from the green on Clifton's historic #1, often rated among the top holes in reviews of area courses. Photo: Courtesy of Jeff Byron.

with a fresh haircut and a clean tee shirt!"

Throughout the park are ballfields, tennis courts, picnic areas and a swimming pool. They are in constant use on weekends by the local community which is entirely black. The golf course remains predominately white. On this day there is no tension in the air as people enjoy the park, doing their thing as we move toward the 21st century.

If you are stout of heart and crave adventure, you get this entire "walk in the park" for only $18.50 including a motorized cart. Camden Yards it ain't — Ebbetts Field it is! You pays your money and you takes your chances.

THE GAME

Baseball is the American way of life. It
is the product of our past colonial masses.
It grew everywhere, in the cities and tiny
hamlets across the nation. As the country
grew the game grew with it. The game molded
the nation. Through waves of immigration,
a World War, national depression, another
World War, the Space Age, Integration,
Vietnam, and the Great Society, baseball
was our glue. . . A yearly passage through the
warm months to the next year. It is the
benchmark of our growth, as individuals,
as families, and as a culture.

Now as we approach the 21st Century, the
game perseveres, moving through time on
an endless path through the fabric of our
lives. It has endured all the frailties
of it's participants. . . scandal, racism,
exploitation, selfishness and crass
commercialism. You can hate its plight, but
you can never turn away from it.

Just like America, baseball will endure.

October 1, 1993

HOW TO WATCH A GAME
Tips to Maximize
Your Understanding & Enjoyment

"18. Look for changes in tempo and strategy after a time out. This is when defenses are adjusted and key substitutions are made."

When you've been around the game of basketball for 50 years, in many capacities, you are bound to pick up a few things. I've learned (especially at Cole Field House over the last 17 years) how to prepare for, watch and enjoy, a game in a big crowded arena, and I thought you might enjoy some of these insights.

1. Pick your games in advance – lineup your group and go! (If you become an ESPN couch potato, you will lose touch.)

2. Read the newspaper preview of the game – be aware of injuries, strategy and the importance of the game.

3. Buy a great sandwich on the way to the game. Avoid the rubber hot dog line and buy your soda from a vendor at the 2:00 mark of the 1st half.

4. Arrive early. Have your designated driver drop you at the door and leave your coats in the car. (If you must carry in your winter coat, make sure your keys and wallet are in your pants pockets.)

5. Buy a program. Know the players' numbers, sizes, backgrounds – become aware of "who they are."

6. Go down to courtside for shoot-arounds and warmups. Get a feel for the players, the lighting and the overall atmosphere.

7. Getting seats facing the team benches is a must. This is the stage upon which the coaches, players and referees interact. The scorer's table is the nerve center of the game.

8. Stay away from the student sections and the pep band. You will enjoy the noise coming at you, but you won't enjoy being in the midst of it.

9. If the arena is not full, change your seat location several times. This way you get the full perspective.

10. Analyze the game at halftime with your friends, but keep the banter down during play – no one talks during the opera.

11. The most exciting spot is courtside – just like ringside at the fights. All the nuances, eye contact, sweating, talking, squeaking shoes, and the roar of the crowd above, are riveting.

12. Sitting up high also has some advantages. Spacing and game motion, shot trajectory, velocity of the passes, plus speed and quickness of the players, are most appreciated up high.

13. Best of both worlds – 10-15 feet up, a little off center. You see the break coming at you and view the halfcourt game in front of you, plus a little of 11 & 12.

14. Observe the point guard, the nerve center of the team. Akin to the quarterback in football, watch him communicate with the coach and mates – on the fly – both offensively and defensively.

15. A poor point guard = sloppy play and bad shot selection. Two poor point guards = a rugby match.

16. Two poor point guards and good defense = poor shooting & supreme ugliness. This is a referee's nightmare,

but you should take it for what it's worth and enjoy it anyway.

17. Pressing defenses change the game. A good one results in an uptempo, a poor one results in easy baskets.

18. Look for changes in tempo and strategy after a time out. This is when defenses are adjusted and key substitutions are made.

19. Watch the inside players posting up and being defended. This is the most physical part of the game and it sets up the outside shooting.

20. The trey has changed the game forever. The strategy, the math, the style – players are always pulling up to shoot.

21. At crunch time watch the super. Invariably he will come into focus for the kill.

22. Make a point to thank whomever got you the tickets. A short note, a phone call or a game program.

23. Read the newspaper account the next day. Compare your mental notes with the reporter.

24. Try to see a game on all levels during a season. This broadens your appreciation of the game.

25. Take a young child to a game. Light Their fire early.

ON THE BUS
Always An Adventure

"The moon appeared around one turn illuminating the lights of a small town down below. Suddenly we realized just how far up this mountain we were."

The University of Baltimore and Wheeling College were certainly classified as low budget operations. However, during my time, both schools traveled by charter bus. Lots of schools, mostly state institutions have the gross misfortune of having to travel in vans and station wagons, wedged in between luggage and equipment like so many olives in a pimento baloney loaf. On a typical trip our players would arrive with study materials, pillows, walkman radios, magazines, newspapers and snacks. And in most cases they had the luxury of spreading out in dual seats. A proverbial "student union" on wheels. Our buses were less than luxurious and a little worse for wear, but they sure beat the hell out of the alternatives.

Having everyone "under one roof" was a plus. I always tried to have a faculty member or booster come along as a guest, the better to spread the word through those communities. The food service always packed us a box lunch with cold beverages. These trips served to unite a team. And from my command post seat behind the driver, with microphone in hand, I could control the environment and the subject matter with a flip of the switch. We always played well on the road. I attribute this to the familial atmosphere and element of control created on the bus. In 74-75 and 75-76 we had outstanding talent at Wheeling College and won 20 plus each season. However, during those years Wheeling was in a budget crunch and we made several trips each year in separate vans. We came to some games not ready to play. Our chemistry was not real good. When athletes are given options, you get different "tugs on the rope." Who knows what it cost us? Conversely it was always bitter and demeaning when your opponents crawled out of those cramped institutional vans and proceeded to kick your ass right in your own living room. When all is said and done, the comraderie fostered on the bus trips always made a long season tolerable and less debilitating on the players and coaches. The coach would get to know his players on a more intimate basis.

Now that I am no longer coaching the bus trips are really missed. I always enjoyed sitting in that front seat with the scouting reports, stats, daily newspapers, and some warm coffee. Greeting everyone to an exciting adventure on the highway of dreams. You see players in their purest moments and vice versa. To this day, the thought of "being a part of a team" is a special memory. Lighting up a cigar and rehashing a victory on a long bus ride home is one of life's most underrated pleasures.

A few memorable trips. . .

1969 - Traveling to Roanoke, on a bitter cold morning, the bus konks out on a lonely stretch of highway outside of Hagerstown. The windows fogged up quickly as we watched the driver trudge through a frozen field to a distant farm house. There were no cell phones in those days. It looked like a scene from Dr. Zhivago. An hour passed as we

214

huddled in our seats fighting the cold. A new bus with a mechanic arrived. It too konked out. But the mechanic managed to repair bus #1 and off we went.

1977 – "The Pizza Hut Classic". In early January, during semester break, we traveled to Shepherd College's Holiday Tournament – in Martinsburg, West Virginia. We were the afterthought, playing in the event with Clarion State, Monmouth College, and the host Shepherd Rams. Coming in late Thursday night for the Friday-Saturday venue, we were in search of food before checking into Motel 81. It was snowing when we pulled up to a darkened Pizza Hut. The bus idled in the lot as I raced up to the door which was already locked. Young kids were cleaning the place. Pressing my nose to the window I did my best Charlie Chaplin pantomime, explaining the bus, hungry people, basketball players, digging into my pockets for money, etc., etc. Being a veteran of these small town early closings for years, I had a knack and a routine down pat. This time it worked. The doors opened, in we went, and the pizza never tasted so good. The juke box heated up and I looked the other way when a few pitchers were ordered. It was a perfect pre-tourney arrival. We were loose. We ate well, made friends, and gave a generous tip. The Pizza Hut kids came to the tournament to root for the Cardinals. We played our best basketball of the year, demolishing a huge Clarion team as talented Monmouth upset the host Rams. In the final we outran Monmouth, scoring over 100 points. After the awards we got on the bus with our trophy and made an after hours stop at the same Pizza Hut. Honored guests, we partied into the night. Everything was free and the hit of the night was Doc Sutherland leading a conga line around the Hut while balancing the trophy on his head.

1978 – In the terrible Winter of 1978 we traveled via Wheeling Rapid Transit (what a misleading name that was) into the bowels of West Virginia for a two game weekend trip. First to Elkins to face Davis & Elkins, then to Bluefield to play Bluefield State in West Virginia's southernmost spot. In 1972 Interstate #79 opened, and for the first time since the Ice Age, West Virginia had a workable North-South venue. Prior to its opening, travel from town to town was an epic journey, especially in Winter. And whenever you strayed off the highway, you were still in God's Country big time. The Wheeling Rapid Transit, which was "going out of business" before our very eyes, had dubious equipment, and maintenance consisted of an oil change and a quick kick of the tires. The latter stage of the trip into Elkins takes you into a downward, corkscrew pattern, seemingly on the way to China. Winning by a few points in that frozen cinder block gym, built by hand after the War by Press Maravich, was rewarding, a hundred spectators not withstanding. The AP Wire sends the score not the message.

Tunneling our way up from Elkins, heading for the mother vein of Interstate #79, a light rain begins to freeze on the windshield. All of a sudden the bloom of victory came off the rose. Only 35 miles away from Weston (hometown of Vic Wojcihovski) as the crow flies, it takes two and a half hours. Turning Southward on #79 the sleet turns to heavy snow. Three hours later we approach the Southern tip of the State. All the players are asleep. It's just me and Freddy, Wheeling Rapid Transit's "one and only" charter driver, coming up on the New River Gorge span. My sons Greg (12) and Nick (10) are also asleep in the front seat. I pray they won't awaken. The New River Gorge Bridge is the largest single arch steel span bridge in the world, nearly 1,000 feet up from the river below and more than a half-mile long. It's the bridge you saw in those soda commercials where the stuntmen parachute over the sides. Nearing the bridge the wind picks up creating a blinding swirl of snow. The bus began to creep across the span. Freddie made a few guttural sounds as both his hands "white knuckled" the wheel. Looking down, the guard rail seemed like a play fence in a Christmas Garden. My face itched and I said a prayer. I thought of the Flying Wallendas crossing the circus tent on a unicycle. I was gripped with fear. We reached the other side, Freddie made a few "whistling in the graveyard" braggadocio cracks. He wasn't fooling me. I knew he wet his drawers on this one.

But things weren't over yet. Just outside of Bluefield we turned off Interstate #19 at Spanishburg. Pipestem State Park was our destination. Located about five miles up a steep mountain it was a beautiful ski resort with reasonable rates and plush accommodations. Only 15 miles outside of Bluefield it was perfect. But on a night like this one, it was fraught with danger. Bluefield, West Virginia, is a town steeped in Baltimore Oriole tradition. Dozens of the team's star players and famous managers played in this old border town, the most notable being Cal Ripken, Jr., who broke into professional baseball later that year and played 63 games for Bluefield. I always wanted to be out of Bluefield right after the game. I can't help but think that this experience helped forge his "streak" mentality.

Making our way up to Pipestem this night would be a

Nearly 1,000 feet above the river, the New River Gorge Bridge is a scary sight on a sunny day, but it is especially terrifying on an icy Winter's night (inset).
Photos: Courtesy of W. Jack Flint, Flint photos, Oak Hill, West Virginia.

tough undertaking. The players were now awake as Freddie goosed the old war horse up and around each turn. By now there were several inches of fresh snow on the ground and you could feel the struggle as the bus would slip, slide, and grab around the turns. The moon appeared around one turn illuminating the lights of a small town down below. Suddenly we realized just how far up this mountain we were. One more turn and the lights of the resort would guide our way. But making the final hairpin turn was too much for the reeling Wheeling war horse. The bus began to slide down the mountain. Furiously working the brakes, turning the wheel, and muttering those guttural sounds, Freddie finally lurched the bus to rest against a snow banked guard rail. We needed no invitation as every passenger quickly chose a fast exit into the stormy night. We climbed the final mile up to Pipestem, leaving the ass end of the bus just a few rotations away from oblivion below. No, this wasn't a Swiss Alpine skiing expedition, just another road trip in the West Virginia Conference. The next night in the Brushfork National Guard Armory we got ourselves another win. The long road back to Wheeling featured a clear, bitter cold, and windy night. There was no heat in the bus as everyone curled up in fetal positions and fought the cold. The mountain wind whistled through every creaking crevice in the war horse. Freddie drove us into the night – wearing a wool pullover army surplus hat, with a scarf and fur mittens – past hollowed strip mines and moon shadowed hills. My friends back East would read the results. The AP Wire sends the score not the message.

THE SPIRIT OF ST. JOSEPH'S MONASTERY
The Flame Will Always Be There

"When walking home from a hot summer day of baseball, a stop in the Monastery was a great "cool off time" for a sweaty 12-year old without a dime for a soft drink. The holy water was always cold."

As we approached the first Christmas in the last decade of the 20th Century (1990), I began to reflect. Time races by. My children are now men. The flow of nature begins to take its toll on relatives, friends, and associates. Funerals, weddings, and special holidays like Christmas take us back to our beginnings. We think of days past. We cling to the memories and warm feelings that have shaped our lives.

The religious zeal and ceremony of youth are gone, but every Christmas season I am drawn back to my childhood.

Driving up the steep hill of Monastery Avenue, a magnificent stone church appears before your eyes. The sight is unexpected, compelling. Rising up from a knoll in Southwest Baltimore, in a blue collar neighborhood called Irvington, it overpowers the small row houses at its doorstep. And regardless of the season or time of day, there is a wind swirling around its edges.

But in the early 1930's, it was home to the Passionist Fathers of Union City, New Jersey. They built a community that was a focal point for the hundreds of parishioners in the 1930's through the 1970's. Behind this church is another connected edifice with a grand steeple and four-sided clock, simply called the "old church." South, through a fenced grove of property, is a large three-story school housing grades one through eight. An adjacent convent for the Sisters of Notre Dame provided us with teachers. This twenty acre enclave, carved out of an old Catholic neighborhood, had two cemeteries by its borders. This was the parish of St. Joseph's Monastery.

In addition to providing the spiritual support for its local parishioners, the Monastery also served as a healing influence for Catholics from all over. The Novenas and Retreats conducted by the Passionist Fathers brought people from the City, surrounding counties and, eventually, by the bus load from bordering states.

The church, located at the corner of Old Frederick Road and Monastery Avenue, is a combination of Gothic and Roman architecture. Built in 1933, the inside remained plain and unfinished. Despite the presence of stained glass, marble floors, and dark oak pews, the spacious interior, with its huge pillars and high walls of brushed mortar, was austere and cold. From the high ceiling hung medieval-style lanterns. On the side walls were scenes depicting the Stations of the Cross. From the outside, the church was powerful and awe inspiring; on the inside, it was another world, dark and peaceful.

The church was always cold. When walking home from a hot summer day of baseball, a stop in the Monastery was a great "cool off time" for a sweaty 12-year old without a dime for a soft drink. The holy water was always cold. In winter, with just the sixth grade class inside for confessions, the church was freezing cold. The nuns always carried their thick wool shawls.

The Passionist Fathers were missionary priests who traveled the earth in search of souls for Christ. Parish work was their training ground. They were not the ordinary secular, parish priests. They heard confessions, preached impassioned sermons, conducted Novenas and Retreats, and said Mass. My, did they say Mass – in Latin, seven days a week. Weekday Masses started at 5:20 a.m.; on Sundays they started at 6:00 a.m. and continued at 7:00, 8:00, 9:00, 10:00 and 11:30. During the holy season of Lent, Mass was also celebrated on the side altars by young Passionist priests who were ordained and still studying at the Monastery, waiting assignment. We called them "student priests." During the late 1940's, the Monastery housed over two dozen priests.

Behind the scenes was a corps of altar boys. Recruited from the parish school, we met every Friday for training and assignments. All prayers at Mass were in Latin. We were drilled in the responses and learned all the moves on the altar

"Driving up the steep hill on Monastery Avenue, a magnificent stone church appears before your eyes." – my childhood memory of the approach to St. Joseph's Monastery. Photo: Courtesy of St. Joseph Monastery Parish

for Mass, weddings, funerals, benedictions, baptisms, Stations of the Cross, and other religious ceremonies.

As money from the parishioners and the outside worshippers began to flow in during the 1950's, a decision to finish the inside of the church was made. It was a huge project that took several years. Michelangelo would have loved the assignment. Every nook and cranny of this huge church was painted. No area escaped. Recreations of the apostles, angels, holy scenes, frescoes and borders, all in bright colors, transformed the place. The already imposing altar was then covered by an enormous marble canopy some thirty feet high. It was shipped piece by piece from Italy. Controversy raged throughout the parish between the purists and the new wave traditionalists, but all should have been pleased that this new beautification, somehow, did not detract from the wood, marble, and stained glass that marked the original personality of the church.

Growing up in this community gave one a sense of security and well being – one that transcended religion. The social, economic and moral overtones of living in this parish were very real. Even though we were in the middle of the 20th Century, our church and parish had an old fashioned magnetism that held it together. It was as if we lived in another time. Coming out of the Depression and into World War II kept people close to the simple things.

The highlight of the year was Christmas Day. The 9 o'clock Children's Mass was a sight to behold. The church was transformed into a paradise of flowers and plants. Large wreaths with the traditional red bows hung from the walls at measured intervals around the church. Garlands of greenery stretched from wreath to wreath forming a bond. The altar was a veritable tropical flower garden with the fragrant smell of majestic white lilies filling the atmosphere.

To the right of the main altar was the larger than life Nativity scene, complete with Wise Men, shepherds and animals, with a blinking ceramic star over the manger.

The church was filled with over 2,000 worshippers. All the children were dressed in their "Sunday Best." The students sat in assigned areas, by class, with their teachers. They were laden with prayer books and hymnals to aid in the responses. On the flowery altar for the Solemn High Mass were the three Passionist celebrants attended by three altar boys. On the sides of the altar were the "student priests," neatly scrubbed, in their black robes and bare sandals. They would come in a procession from the back of the altar, chanting in Latin, each carrying a candle. Kneeling at the foot of the altar were six young altar boys clad in red, white and gold cassocks. They would serve as acolytes during the Communion. Two other altar boys attended the burning of incense. This surrealistic scene of "Old World Religion" played out before you in a colorful panorama of drama. It made you think of times gone by – of the Bible, of saints, of ancient peoples, of God and Who He must be; and of the millions of people who witnessed and professed during the same ritual in which you were now partaking. It was heavy stuff.

As the Mass unfolded, the main celebrant would chant the prayers in Latin. The student priests would respond in resonant acapellas, their voices filling the church. All the while, the smell of fresh flowers mingled with the sweet aroma of incense. The choir would sing the Christmas songs in Latin and English. The Communion would be signalled by the gentle tinkle of bells. The acolytes with lighted candles would proceed to the steps of the altar as the celebrant raised the host on high. When the assemblage began its movement to the rail, other priests appeared to serve the Communion. The altar was alive with costumed figures moving through the garden of flowers and the haze of incense. The quiet procession of Holy Communion had begun in earnest.

Organ music filled the air. From the choir came the Latin hymn, Panis Angelicus (Bread of the Angels), and for a moment in time, on a Christmas Day past but never forgotten, a little piece of what Heaven must be like descended upon me. All the traditions instilled from birth crystallized themselves in that one brief moment at Holy Communion.

If all that religion has become is illusion and memories, so be it. But to anyone of any faith who has experienced such a moment, the flame will always be there. It is simply called "belief in a Supreme Being." Although this ritual may never be repeated in my lifetime, I always know I can return to the Monastery on a Christmas Day for spiritual sustenance. All the pomp and circumstance are gone now. A single priest and an attendant are all that remain on most Sundays, but the memory and spark of that spirit will always remain with me. It is a gift I received long ago, never to be forgotten.

And as I close, for all people everywhere, may the spirit of Christ be with you always.

INDEX